Calvin Johansson has had wide and varied experience in the ministry of music including duty in the armed service as organist and choral director of the Post Chapel at West Point Military Academy, as a minister of music, and as a college choral director. A graduate of Houghton College, Union Theological Seminary, and Southwestern Baptist Theological Seminary, Dr. Johansson is presently a professor of music at Evangel College. He resides in Springfield, Missouri with his wife and two children.

MUSIC & MINISTRY

A Biblical Counterpoint

Calvin M. Johansson

HENDRICKSON
PUBLISHERS
PEABODY, MASSACHUSETTS 01961-3473

Dedicated to my teachers at Houghton, Union, and Southwestern
and to the
teaching ministry of the church musician.

3rd Printing March, 1988

Copyright © 1984 by Hendrickson Publishers, Inc.
P.O. Box 3473, Peabody, MA 01961-3473

ISBN: 0-913573-07-8

Table of Contents

PROLOGUE   iii

CHAPTER ONE: PHILOSOPHICAL PERSPECTIVES   3

I.   Philosophical Discernment   3
II.   Aestheticism   4
III.   Pragmatism   5
IV.   Biblical Counterpoint   7

CHAPTER TWO: THE DOCTRINE OF CREATION   9

I.   Creation, Dependence, and Independence   9
II.   The Material World and Form   10
III.   *Creatio Continua* and the Church   11
IV.   Creativity   15
V.   Church Nurture of Creativity   16
VI.   Summary: Creative Worth and a Church Imperative   18

CHAPTER THREE: THE *IMAGO DEI*   21

I.   The Broad *Imago Dei*   21
II.   The Narrow *Imago Dei*   24
III.   Summary: Musical Imaging   27

CHAPTER FOUR: THE INCARNATION   30

I.   Divine and Artistic Incarnation   30
II.   Pastoral Humility   31
III.   Communication, Relevance, and Content   34
IV.   Summary   41

CHAPTER FIVE: THE GOSPEL AND CONTEMPORARY CULTURE   42

I.   Music as Witness   42
II.   Gospel Characteristics   43
III.   Mass Culture   47
IV.   The Church and Mass Culture   49
V.   Pop Music Characteristics   50
VI.   The Church and Pop   56
VII.   Methodological Questions   58
VIII. Folk Music and Jazz   59
IX.   Summary: An Urgent Theological Resolve   62

CHAPTER SIX: FAITH   63

I.   The Wholeness of the Christian Church   63
II. Intellectual and Emotional Imbalances in Church Music   68
III. Faith Action and Tendency Gratification   71
IV. Summary and Congregational Methodology   75

CHAPTER SEVEN: STEWARDSHIP   76

I.   Motivations for Stewardship   76
II. Stewardship's Scope   77
III. Doing One's Best—Principle One   79
IV. Some Dangers   80
V.   Growth—Principle Two   83
VI. Church Music Education   86
VII. A Contrapuntal Dynamic   87

CHAPTER EIGHT: MYSTERY AND AWE   89

I.   Music and Ministry   89
II. Truth and Musical Composition   92
III. Beyond the Explicitness of Words   96
IV. Imparting a Sense of Mystery   99
V.   Summary   101

CHAPTER NINE: CONCLUSION   102

I.   The Crucifixion   102
II. The Resurrection   104
III. A Contrapuntal Dynamic   107
IV. Application: A Working Counterpoint   111

NOTES   22

BIBLIOGRAPHY   129

INDEX   134

Prologue

Of necessity, the church musician is a zealous, eager, and energetic worker who has little time for reflection, contemplation, and philosophic thought. What he most often craves is inspiration, new ideas, repertoire, methodological suggestions, problem solving, and technical review.

Yet here is a book that asks music directors, pastors, choir members, soloists, instrumentalists, organists, and pianists to set aside their music making momentarily and to reflect seriously on their activities—a brief sabbatical for reviewing Biblical principles foundational to music ministry.

Such reflection will have a practical outcome, for it is our thinking that determines what our specific actions will be: choice of music, performance preparation, and congregational concern. The time spent in thoughtfully considering a Biblical perspective on church music will be justified as our vision is clarified, enlarged, and deepened. The workaday world will thus find a new music nourished and shaped by a theological repast too often missing in our busy lives.

The pastoral music ministry, as opposed to the evangelistic, missionary, or other music ministry, is the field of inquiry in these pages. This is not to say that the principles valid for pastoral orientation would automatically be invalidated when applied to other music ministries, but certain emphases would be changed. For our purposes we shall concern ourselves only with the music program of the local church—the pastoral ministry of music.

A vital point must now be made that is critical to understanding the following pages—that is, *no single doctrine or theological topic is intended to stand alone.* Each needs the others in a contrapuntal dynamic. As in musical counterpoint, such a contrapuntal "discussion" acknowledges the right of each theological "theme" to exist independently in its own right. Yet it is only as these independent themes are harmonized by combining them in disciplined relationship that music, or in our case fuller truth, will be forthcoming. What is said about creation and creativity in Chapter 2, for example, can only be understood in the light of every other chapter. This is important to remember, for then the apparent contradictions that exist between many of these themes will be seen as illuminating the various sides of our large and multi-faceted subject. Readers who wish a further explanation of this method before beginning Chapter 1 may refer to Chapter 9, section III, "A Contrapuntal Dynamic."

Approaching our theological topics contrapuntally (in relationship with one another, as it were) will keep one from hasty, naive, and simplistic solutions that serve only to emphasize one side of the truth. These doctrinal themes will come together in the last chapter in a counterpoint whose design will affirm grace, integrity, and even practicality, and which will shun legalistic rules and harsh rigidity. Meanwhile, many volatile matters are dealt with in a forthright manner in accordance with the subject of the moment. No apology is made for the direct approach taken. These issues must be faced openly, honestly, and with a certain Biblical ruggedness.

We proceed!

c o u n—t e r—p o i n t

a process of musical conversation

1

PHILOSOPHICAL PERSPECTIVES

I. Philosophical Discernment

The church musician called to a pastoral ministry of music has a most reward-ing vocation ahead of him. It is rewarding because of his people's pilgrimage in those things most important in life, values with eternal significance. He deals with much more than music.

As in all ministries, the practical working out of his calling as a Christian, pastor, and artist-musician is not as easy as it might seem at first glance. In-deed, the variety of pressures from his congregation, minister, choir, church board, music committee, and colleagues is enormous. Then too, he must deal with his own conscience, his own prophetic vision, lessons from history, and his ongoing professional maturity. His course becomes increasingly difficult to control as the winds of opposing points of view batter and toss him about like the proverbial ship without a rudder. Disorientation, lack of a clearly defined goal, and uncertainty about his methodology result.

The fact is that, confusion or not, Sundays roll around in a steady, unhalting procession. There are choices to be made concerning the required comple-ment of instrumental, vocal, and congregational music. Will it be Bach, Peter-son, Palestrina, Lovelace, Burroughs, Vaughn Williams, Gaither, Crosby, Zim-merman, or a combination of these? We must choose something, and the choice we make reflects our thinking. One's music fleshes out one's intent. Even those who deny any musical, theological, or philosophical value system base their decisions on some value system—even that of no system. Inevitably we choose; inevitably we judge the music we use in the light of our philosophy, whatever it may or may not be. The only sure defense against fruitless and unprofitable wanderings is sound thinking. It is a critical necessity in choos-ing music that every church musician formulate a solid underlying philosophical rationale that is coherent, comprehensive, and creative. The working out of his calling is at stake.

The key point is that the church musician must have a valid base from which to work. If we cannot avoid choices, and they are made as a result of our philosophical position, admitted or not, it is imperative that we give atten-tion to the formulation of credible guiding principles. We cannot afford to be haphazard, careless, or indiscriminate in coming to grips with the issues.

It is not a matter of having a philosophy (we all have one) or choosing what best suits our needs and the expediency of the moment. It is a matter of wrestling with the substantive alternatives until we are compelled to adopt a position that not only agrees with revealed truth but also enthusiastically promulgates that truth in all its fullness.

II. Aestheticism

Generally, church musicians base decisions about their programs on two common philosophies: aestheticism and pragmatism. Aestheticism is concerned with the technical characteristics found in the music which give to it its artistic worth and hence its supposed worth as church music. For example:

> The rhythm should have life and movement without levity, and dignity without heaviness. The melody of all the parts, not of the treble only, should be shapely in outline, and neither angular nor dull; in general it should be diatonic, and chromatic intervals should be only sparingly used. The harmony should be for the most part simple, avoiding excessive use of discords which introduce a note of vulgarity or triviality, and which pall with repetition.[1]

Archibald Davison, in *Protestant Church Music in America*, lists seven theoretical elements of music that must be shaped in certain ways to produce music that is free of secular associations and of high enough quality to warrant use in church.[2] Aestheticism treats church music first and last as an art; its whole purpose is simply to be beautiful. By careful attention to aesthetic values, both composer and listener can be assured of the quality of artistry necessary for the worship of Almighty God.

However, there are three problems with aestheticism as a philosophical basis for church music. First, aesthetic analysis, like music theory, comes after the fact. Artistry cannot be automatically assumed by confining creative output to the following of theoretical rules deduced from what has been done. Aesthetic insights are valuable as guideposts and are useful (depending on the particular system) as a check on musical quality, but legalistic regulations for the management of music in the church are doomed to failure. If church music is to flourish, there needs to be a philosophical base that goes beyond legalism.

Second, a perusal of aesthetic theories shows that as a branch of philosophy, aesthetics is concerned with explaining beauty within a given system of thought. Art is part of the reality of our world and the philosopher must make room for it in his system. Yet there is no way to insure that one's sensitivity to artistic values will be enhanced by an analysis of the beautiful. Many philosophers who give lengthy explanations of beauty do not have a very high personal regard for the arts. Aesthetics, then, used methodologically, cannot guarantee an improvement in musical taste and hence has little educational worth for promoting musical growth and maturity.

A third problem with aestheticism is the danger of artistic veneration. One becomes completely engrossed in musical beauty for the wrong reasons. The art becomes an end in itself; it selfishly destroys any other rival. After a lifetime of study in the field of aesthetics, DeWitt Parker, an American aesthetician, said of religion and art:

> For these stories, even when believed, have an existence in the imagination precisely comparable to that of works of art, and their influence upon sentiment is of exactly the same order. They are most effective when beautiful, as the legends of Christ and Buddha are beautiful; and they function by the sympathetic transference of attitude from the story to the believer. Even when no longer accepted as true their influence may persist, for the values they embody lose none of their compulsion. And, although as an interpretation of life based upon faith religion is doubtless eternal, its specific forms are probably all ficticious; hence each particular religion is destined to pass from the sphere of faith to that of art. The Greek religion has long since gone there, and there also a large part of our own will someday go—what is lost for faith is retained for beauty.[3]

Charles T. Smith thought of music and religion in a similar way:

> Now a church is like a theatre, and as soon as the service begins we are conscious of entering a world of illusion or make-believe in which the creed and ritual of any religion appear to be logically developed and, to that extent, satisfying to the intellect, because a religion is a work of art. It may be based upon the most incredible tenets, but if it is given good constructive form, fashioned with competent craftsmanship—which is usually the case with institutional religions which have an elaborate ritual—it is identical with an immense play . . . Religion is indeed, like music, an art; and a system of theology, like a system of music, is, as Dr. Charles Singer claims, "As much the product of human ingenuity as a motor car."[4]

In building upon aesthetics as the foundation for a philosophy of church music, we run the risk of elevating art to a place where beauty becomes God, or if not thought to be God, is at least equal to God, or thought of as essential to knowing God. Although there are values in an assessment of the aesthetic experience for arguing the existence of God,[5] there can be no justification for placing art in a position where it may become that which is worshipped. We worship the Creator, not the created—God, not beauty.

The dangers of aestheticism are clear. At the very least, its nebulous, analytical passivity does not necessarily encourage a creative dynamic; at most, it is idolatrous.

III. Pragmatism

The other philosophy that often serves as a foundation for music ministry is pragmatism. "For church music the standard must be primarily a practical one . . . good church music is that which does most effectively what it is supposed to do."[6] Function is everything.[7] Music becomes a tool to do things to people. The overriding concern, sought after at any cost, is the achieving of a predetermined result. This result (end) justifies the use of any music (means) as long as the anticipated result is worthy. In the ethical realm, for example, lying, cheating, and stealing are justified when the goal is a noble one. Likewise in the artistic realm, doing away with musical goodness, integrity, and truth is completely justified when the intended result is a meritorious one. Compositional standards become non-entities—categories which are no longer valid, indeed which no longer exist. A pragmatist does not judge music itself to be either good or bad. Its goodness or badness lies totally in its ability to bring the results assigned to it. The motto of the pragmatic music director is "I'll do anything to get the message across."

However, as a foundation for music ministry, pragmatism fares no better than aestheticism. In the first place, pragmatism falsely creates a sharp dichotomy between medium and message, music and gospel, in which each may go its own way without regard for the other. Such a separation of means and ends effectively destroys the more useful premise that for gospel witness, ends ought to determine means. How one communicates should be dictated by what one communicates. The music and the message should be organically related. The pragmatist is unconcerned that the two may be in conflict. He uses music uncritically as a message lubricator, sweetener, or psychological conditioner. Regardless of its contraposition to the message itself, whatever music will make the acceptance of the message easier, more palatable, and as reflexive as possible, that music is adopted. The pragmatist, in his concern for communication, emasculates the gospel in his dependence upon a commercialized system of music to sell his message. The gospel is stripped of its full integrity and power, and manipulative selling technique supplants the work of the Spirit.

Second, pragmatism does away with objective standards. One cannot talk about a "good" or "bad" composition as a piece of music. Its "goodness" or "badness" is thought of in terms of the results it brings. In denying authority, music that has no accountability for value, no standards save acceptability, and no quality control except results, cannot be considered an art form at all. It loses its integrity, inherent worth, and freedom to speak. Forcing the medium to give up its characteristic identity is to use it as a prostitute. Pragmatism paves the way for an absurdist world-view in which standards, authority, and prophetic purpose are absent.

Third, pragmatism shows its proclivity toward philosophical self-destruction. Elton Trueblood, noting that pragmatism's insidious influence has crept far beyond the parameter of scholarship into everyday life, says:

> The crucial fallacy of pragmatism is the falsity of its own inner contradiction. It appears to uphold the idea that all truth is relative, but relative to what? Since it cannot say "relative to objective truth," it is forced to make pragmatism itself its center of reference. A brilliant critic of pragmatism in history has pointed this out in the following passage. Professor Commanger's plea is a plea that we should conform to something, i.e. the pragmatic idea. He refers to what he calls 'the first lesson of pragmatism: damn the absolute!' but at the same time he is himself pleading that we should receive the pragmatic ideal as if it were an absolute. The philosophy that damns the absolute is strangely revealed as the

absolute philosophy.'' *The Bent World,* J.V. Langmead Casserly. (New York: Oxford University Press, 1955), p. 122.
To make a new absolute out of the doctrine that there is no absolute is obvious confusion.[8]

Thus the pragmatic base so popular with church musicians for establishing a working philosophy of music is found wanting. It dilutes the gospel by allowing the music to be separate from and unaffected by Biblical discipline; it naively supports a world-view in which the absence of objective musical standards often leads to or is symptomatic of the erosion of a widely sweeping Biblical authority; and it logically destroys itself through its own internal inconsistencies.

Aestheticism and pragmatism, though, are seldom carried through in a complete and systematic way. Pragmatism may take from the aesthetic a remote and contorted regard for musical quality; aestheticism often draws from the pragmatic a chafing and distasteful recognition of the necessity of being practical and success-oriented in a very ''unidealistic'' world.

However, the shifting back and forth of values, standards, and directions produces a philosophic unrest which prohibits the carrying out of all that a ministry of music could and should be. As already noted, without a coherent, comprehensive, and creative basic philosophy, a church music program is like a rudderless ship driven by a shifting wind. Confusion reigns.

IV. Biblical Counterpoint

We have established the inescapability of having a philosophy, the need for a credible working philosophy of music, and the necessity of rejecting aestheticism and pragmatism. That leaves us with the question: What will constitute the basis of our judgments?

It would seem that a profitable line of inquiry concerning music in the church would be to develop a foundation based on the church's distinctive— an allegiance to truth as revealed in Holy Scripture. Erik Routley has shown that Biblical truth as formulated in theological principles is of paramount importance in addressing the problems of music in the church.[9] Biblical truth speaks to all situations.

If theology is to be the foundation of our value system, we should expect that the musician's regard for his art cannot by definition become idolatrous. By the same token, methodology will not be worshipped. His means will be determined by his theological presuppositions. He will not bow at the shrine of success. There will be no conflict between artistry, spirituality, and methodology.

In the theological realm, the finite mind can best understand truth within the tension of apparent opposites. God cannot be contained by propositional statements. As soon as we think we have discovered all revealed truth, we discover something else that does not negate our previous understanding but widens it, even though it may seem contradictory. Jesus was fully human yet fully God. God is immanent yet transcendent. He is sovereign yet permissive. Therefore our limited understanding speaks about God in dynamic paradoxes—musically put, a counterpoint.

Methodologically, it is imperative that we note the creative tension apparent in the discovery of Biblical truth, for it is precisely this type of tension that is at the heart of a dynamic and creative church music. In our quest for a workable philosophy we will discover many seeming contradictions, each standing alone in its rightness but showing fuller truth in relationship to the others—a beautiful contrapuntal design which is the philosophical basis of a pastoral music ministry.

2

THE DOCTRINE OF CREATION

I. Creation, Dependence, and Independence

The doctrine of creation is fundamental to both theological and artistic realms. As Langdon Gilkey puts it, God's creatorship is "the indispensable foundation on which the other beliefs of the Christian faith are based."[1] This doctrine also supports the whole artistic enterprise. God as creator has given creative gifts to humanity: the artistic raw material of our world, personal creative ability, and the compulsion to create in freedom. Man's creative ability is totally derived from God, for without Him all things would cease. It would seem logical, then, to set in motion an investigation of this doctrine, which holds together, and is inextricably linked with, both theology and art. Its natural priority in the scheme of things is an indication of its fundamental importance for church music philosophy.

To begin, God creates *ex nihilo*. He creates out of nothing. He originates absolutely that which was not. His creation is not the mere rearrangement of finite elements but the creation of those elements that never were. He imagines the unimaginable and creates the uncreatable. He creates in freedom and His creating is supernatural, mysterious, and purposeful. It is the ultimate uniqueness. Moreover, that which is exists only as He sustains it, though the Creator is entirely separate from that which He creates.

Man, on the other hand, cannot create *ex nihilo* and is therefore dependent upon God and the created order. Whatever man makes, the raw material—be it sound, color, or stone—already exists; the artist merely reorganizes these God-given elements into some meaningful reality.

> In the truest sense artists do not 'create,' they can only represent, symbolize, or translate what is given. At best they can take materials such as pigment, stone, words, or musical symbols, and rearrange them in such a way as to give communicable impressions of their ideas.[2]

While there are those who hold that the artist is an autonomous maker, our presupposition is that no matter what man says, artistic creation is irrevocably bound to the material stuff which God has created. Even man's own life is dependent on God the Creator and Sustainer, so that all men, even composers, performers, and listeners, are absolutely and utterly dependent.

On the other hand, certain independence is needed in order to create works of art. Man, created in freedom by God, is a recipient of God-given freedom, has a free will, and is responsible for his own free activity. For example, freedom in decision-making is the basis of human personality and involves "adding qualities and dimensions to personality that simply were not there, and would not be there now, apart from the free act."[3] There is a sense here that something new, fresh, and unique is emerging. So it is in the making of artistic work. The artist's autonomous decisions that are made in composing a piece of music bring freely into being that which has not existed. Thus while man is incapable of creating in the primal sense, he does have the capability of creating unique works. Only in this limited sense can we assert that man creates *ex nihilo* and is independent of his Maker.

Man's making is thus dependent on pre-existent stuff, yet the decisions required for all that goes into the creative act show his independence. Man must rely both on God and on himself. He is dependent yet independent. Consequently, the church musician as an artist will acknowledge his dependence and create in humility, for all that he does in music making is a gift of a loving God. He cannot treat his gift haughtily or lightly, but reverently and seriously.

Since the musician is also independent in his creating, he has a certain exaltedness. His artistic sovereignty is absolute. The autonomy necessary to create, recreate, and appreciate the vehicle of his pastoral calling, namely music, is a necessary part of his creative humanity. He alone is responsible for his decisions. As a creator he stands independently on his own feet.

The church artist, more than any other person, should realize the implications of such a contrapuntal stance. The artist, being independent yet dependent, relying on himself yet on God, and creating in freedom yet being bound, is caught in the tension between his humility and his exaltedness. The balance achieved in the creative application of these opposites will give a proper perspective to the music ministry. On the one hand there will be utter reliance on the Almighty and a tendency for self-deprecation; on the other hand there will be personal initiative and, in the right sense, pride in fulfilling individual capabilities. He must exist in a "humble exaltedness" which will allow him to be an open channel, without abasement or arrogance, full of creativity resulting from a cooperative venture between God and man.

II. The Material World and Form

The doctrine of creation affirms the goodness of the material world, for nothing in the world which God has created is intrinsically evil. This conclusion does not mean that the world is perfect; it too is inexplicably involved in the Fall and eventually is to be redeemed. Nevertheless, the material world is a gift from God, has potential, and is fundamentally good.[4] Consequently the artist must respect it.

The doctrine also suggests that creation was purposeful; that is, in imposing form upon chaos and order upon confusion, God manifested purpose, the process of form-giving being an intrinsically purposive action. Moreover, His motivation was and is exclusively love, divine love, carried out within the context of divine freedom. Thus, to say, "God creates" is to say that in freedom He lovingly gives form to purpose.

This orderliness, or form, woven into the fabric of the universe is a basic principle found in all creation and is a requirement for artistic intelligibility. At the bottom of creation is design, not chaos, and music as part of the created order of our world must participate in the laws of our existence. Artistic musical form shows forth the orderliness and purposefulness of God's creation. Without coherence, shape, purpose, or "form," there is no music.

Much contemporary philosophic thought scorns the idea of order in our world. Themes such as "Life is absurd," Existence is meaningless," and "Man is a mere vegetable" are common. In an art such as music, which lacks the definitive symbols of language, the same philosophy of meaninglessness, absurdity, and purposelessness can be communicated through lack of form. For example, believing that "Simple minds cling to the illusion of an orderly, purposeful universe because it gives them a sense of security,"[5] John Cage musically expresses the philosophy of the absurdity of meaning in life through the aleatory (chance) process of musical composition. There is no coherence, shape, meaning, or form to it. Musically he shows the world and all therein to be accidental, purposeless, and chaotic—the product of chance.

However, an allegiance to the Biblical doctrine of creation, which holds that God imposed form upon formlessness, that the world has purpose and meaning (which is to say, a goal, form, or direction), and that the material world is good, demands that the creative artist's work mirror reality. Man craves wholeness, and art and religion both deal with reality in a holistic manner. Without the universal artistic ingredient of form, music ceases to be art because it has no goal or purpose. In reflecting the philosophy of purposelessness, aleatory music is absolutely useless for any kind of positive affirmation concerning the real world and is therefore worthless as church music. It is incumbent upon musicians to be aware of the artistic qualities that give music its coherence and shape. Music that hangs together well affirms this aspect of the doctrine of creation; music that is chaotic because it lacks coherent form denies the doctrine.

III. *Creatio Continua* and the Church

The doctrine of creation is concerned not only with the original purposeful bringing into being of matter out of nothing, *creatio ex nihilo,* but also with God's care and sustenance of the world, *creatio continua.* The world itself and everything in it is continuously supported by the ongoing process of creation. This doctrine contends that the work of creation is never finished, unlike the view that God created a world which, like the watchmaker's watch after having been wound, is self-reliant and functions independently of its Maker. *Creatio continua* states that the maintenance of our world is the continuance of creation and cannot be separated from it. "To say that he has created involves saying that he is creating now. To sustain is to continue to create, not merely to maintain that which has been created."[6] Ongoing creation, then, is very much a part of our existence. Without God, our world would cease to exist; therefore, since He is immanent, He still shapes and moves the world toward the destiny He has chosen for it.

Creatio continua is partially man's responsibility. God ordered that man be appointed an agent of His continuing creative activity. In the book of Genesis, man's responsibility is referred to as "having dominion over the earth" and is, in fact, the book's dominant theme.[7] As a duty, dominion-having is central to man's existence, for it is woven into the very warp and woof of his being. This responsibility given to man to "subdue" the earth and to have dominion over it has been called by theologians the *creation mandate*. This divine charge calls all men to live out their creaturely existence creatively and fully.

The mandate to fulfill the potential of this world through the creativity of mankind is an important responsibility, but the task is not greater than the God-given ability for accomplishment. All men are by nature wonderers, imaginers, and inventors, though in their fallen state they need to be reminded again and again that they do not automatically live creatively. Effort is required. They need a far-sighted vision of what the world might become and the will to implement their vision. In thus fulfilling the creation mandate, man becomes an arm of God's *creatio continua,* His continuing creation.

Not only was mankind given a mandate for the general care and development of the world, but a cultural mandate was given as well.

> Implicit in the doctrine of creation, then, is its cultural mandate and the call to a creative integration of faith with learning and culture. It is a call . . . to explore the wisdom of God in every area of thought and life, and to replenish the earth with the creativity of human art and science.[8]

Emil Brunner illuminates this point of man's responsibility for cultural development when he says:

> The capacity for culture and the desire for culture are characteristic marks of the Divine creation of humanity. Hence culture [art, education, science, etc.] is both God's gift and man's appointed duty; it is a gift, in so far as man cannot help creating culture, and it is a duty, in so far as apart from it he has no right to exist, because otherwise he does not realize his God-given purpose in creation.[9]

Men are not merely to accept uncritically the cultural environment in which they live, but are to take action in making it what it could and should be. To form and fashion the world culturally is part of their responsibility.

The cultural mandate is a call faced by every artist. He is neither to withdraw from the world nor only to please, entertain, and profit selfishly from his creative work. His primary purpose is to take the stuff of creation and incarnate it into a meaningful form that speaks deeply and powerfully of the fundamental but often invisible truths of our existence: birth, life, death, tension, release, relationship, tragedy, ecstasy, newness, eternity, suffering, sound, silence, redemption, and so on. The artist is not to be an idler in the world but a prophet. He has a God-given mission to fulfill by influencing, shaping, and directing the values and vision of culture.

Furthermore, culture is not anti-religious, nor is it neutral, nor is it the same thing as religion. Culture is the mode of living here and now in the world of the Fall. Although it is part of culture, religion transcends culture, impacting it with a supernatural message which should include in its proclamation a certain tender, loving concern for the cultural realm. Cultural development is well within the scope of the church's active concern.

Consequently, the church musician, because he is a person and because he is an artist, must be concerned that the church take seriously its part in actively fulfilling the creation and cultural mandates in our world. He actually has no choice if his ministry is to be all that it should be, for "Art creates culture; it creates values and meanings by which a society fulfills its destiny . . . ''[10] The church musician cannot afford to sit idly by, leaving the formation and direction of culture to the unregenerate. The doctrine of creation, if it is to be believed and lived, means that the church will be in the forefront of artistic activity. Taking the cultural directive seriously would revolutionize church music in that the church body would welcome rather than reject that which has made the true artist often unpopular in church circles. The music director could readily fulfill his prophetic role by helping people see and hear far more than they are comfortable with. The visionary integrity of the individual artist and the visionary integrity of a particular church music program could do much to encourage other church bodies to live out their corporate life creatively and with artistic integrity. Enthusiasm for such prophetic musical ministry would change the artistic climate of the church from an often inflexible conventionality to a flexible originality. The cultural mandate to explore, develop, and create would become a way of life. The church would literally become a community of creators.

The cultural mandate, coming from the broader and more general creation mandate, has a similar sense of continuing creation. Cultural development cannot be cut off from the doctrine of creation, for *creatio continua* is just as real in the cultural realm as in the natural realm: God continues to create by preserving, utilizing, and developing that which He has created through man as co-creator.

Cultural *creatio continua* speaks to the need for remembering and understanding the past as a very necessary guide for new creation. Past creativity must not go unnoticed or uninterpreted so that there might be wisdom in charting an orderly and progressive cultural path. In contrast to the Greek cyclical views, Christianity maintains that there is historical progress in the world. The Hebrew-Christian world view affirms that God reveals Himself to men in terms of real flesh-and-blood events in time. In Acts 10 and 13, Peter and Paul do not give metaphysical discourses but recite a story (i.e., historical events). The Christian religion is a faith primarily grounded in past events and the continuation of that faith is a matter of remembering and interpreting those events. "In short, He [God] is the *Lord of history,* working through men and nations whom He has raised up to fulfill His purpose."[11]

The church has a definite mission under the cultural mandate to preserve man's cultural heritage for the present and the future. It must promote a positive stance toward the immense store of man's inheritance as we use it with gratitude as the basis for the ongoing process of cultural creation for which we are responsible. We should regard history neither as a limit beyond which we cannot go, nor as an unessential which we may disregard.

> The man who would live only out of the "now" is surely as immature as he
> who would regress into the past; and after all, amnesia is a worse sickness than
> nostalgia. Man does not live by the present alone, neither does he live by the
> future alone, and to reject tradition is simply to dismember the self. As memory
> is necessary to the sanity of personality, so tradition sustains the collective per-
> sonality of a people.[12]

Music has a vital function in the church's preservation of its specific heritage
and that of the wider cultural heritage. As we have stated, a primary purpose
of Christianity is to make the past real, and music can be a means to that
end. The church music program must neither stifle nor neglect that music
which belongs to another age. The cultural mandate again makes it imperative
that the church preserve the past because of its responsibility for man's cultural
heritage and because of the historical nature of the church itself. The links
and ties to the past, the communion of saints, and the very important realization that the Christian church has a historical heritage that nourishes the present, are important reasons for using great music of the past in the church
service.

We must avoid an "either/or" situation relative to old and new music.
"Exclusive commitment to a liturgical-musical past imprisons the church in
its past history. Exclusive commitment to an often vapid present imprisons
the church in a rootless now."[13] Cultural *creatio continua* is a matter of treating
the past, present, and future as a unit. A music program should bring a balance
and an integration to the entire store of man's musical creativity.

Historical *creatio continua* also speaks to the artist as a creator. In the finest
sense of the term, the artist is a traditionalist. That is, the artist ought to
build upon his artistic heritage as he explores new possibilities.

> [Tradition involves] in the first place, the historical sense, . . . and the historical
> sense involves a perception, not only of the pastness of the past, but of its presence;
> the historical sense compels a man to write not merely with his own generation
> in his bones, but with a feeling that the whole of the literature of Europe from
> Homer and within it the whole of the literature of his own country has a
> simultaneous existence and composes a simultaneous order. This historical sense
> of the timeless as well as of the temporal and of the timeless and of the temporal
> together, is what makes a writer (or an artist in any field) traditional.[14]

So tradition forms a base of operations, the place from which new horizons
spring. The composer works with one face toward the past and one toward
the future, influenced by history and by the developing art of his own time.
If the composer gets too far from tradition in his contemporary musical
development, his music will have little else but shock value. Historically, it
is difficult to find a composer who isolated himself from the past who was
vindicated later as the true prophet of his time. It is implicit in creation that
one cannot profitably discard tradition. God does not intend that man should
ignore his past but rather that he should build upon it as the evolutionary
process of culture, *creatio continua,* goes on.

IV. Creativity

At this point in our discussion it can be said that man creates as a result of the responsibility cast upon him in the creation mandate. Formed by God, every man is given the task of responding to His call to be a co-creator. We are to be creative as God is creative. The musician employed by a church is not exempt from this call, for under the cultural mandate he too has a mission to fulfill. We shall further develop this when we deal with the *imago Dei,* but for now, suffice it to say that as an artist and as a man he must design his music program to encourage the full development and use of the best creative gifts he and his people have to offer. In response to the Creator's call, the church body will join the music director to fulfill this creative potential.

Creative, creating, and *creativity* are words often nebulously used in conjunction with some vague idea of the new, the novel, or the different, usually without qualitative considerations. The loose usage of these terms makes it difficult to be precise in talking about such a topic as "creation." Thus, our use of these words in this text will mean *that which breaks new ground imaginatively and with integrity.* To be "creative," then, means to originate with artistic excellence.

Such a definition is imperative when we look at God's creation as a model. His imagination is boundless and that which He creates is not shoddy or poorly made. True, we cannot create as God creates, and our activity cannot be directly analogical to His, but we can see in God's creation an example and a directive that man is to create with purpose, meaning, and a sense of imaginative individuality. The beauty of nature gives us a clue as to the direction man's creativity should take. Wherever we look, from the full breadth of the landscape down to the microscopic cell, we see beauty and order without exact duplication of anything. Our own creation will be but a shadow of this heavenly creation, but it is absolutely mandatory that it be at least a shadow. Whenever man is selfish, petty, lazy, indifferent, small, or unconcerned, his creative activity is far from being what God intended.

The essence of musical creativity is to give worthy form to new idea, both of which come through the imagination. That which has not been done before is the musician's domain. "Music which sounds old-fashioned when it is new is almost always valueless because it is bound to be derivative."[15] By this, Gordon Jacob means that the work is essentially a copy, lacking in creative vitality. It is the essential ingredient of imagination which distinguishes fancy from idea, making from craftsmanship. Imagination fares best when it is disciplined and cultivated, and it is helpless in pure fantasy, needing the direction of the intellect. Good imaginative musical ideas are capable of artistic development, and good imaginative craftsmanship develops those ideas so imaginative newness is clearly and profoundly articulated for all to see and hear. Samuel Coleridge saw imagination as a force which is analogous to God's original creation in the forming of new realities. If we interpret the word *analogous* to mean "similar in principle but not the same as," we can agree.

Imagination is the womb in which the creative seed is conceived and developed. It is the quality that is the lifeblood of the entire artistic realm; without it there is no art.

The creative act has two general phases, the subjective (that which is intuitive) and the objective (that which is crafted). The first is a matter of the creative unconscious, the idea; the second is a matter of giving good form to or of incarnating the idea. Of course both are linked together differently with each artist and in a way which even the artist may not be able to explain. One cannot reduce the matter to a formula. It is interesting to note that when Renoir was asked about his artistic procedures, he stated that not a single process could be reduced to a formula, including the amount of oil he added to the paint on his palette.[16] One may be able to assimilate technique and skill but still not be able to compose. On the other hand, excellent intuitive artistic ideas alone are no guarantee that worthy composition will result. There is a certain dependence between intuition and the rules of making. They work together. Concerning this process, Archie J. Bahm says:

> One of the sanest, and most astute, evaluations of the various factors involved in creativity, and specifically artistic creativity, is that by Dr. Walter Gotshalk: "In summing up this analysis of artistic creation, we might say that the total creative process embraces a subjective phase and an objective phase, both environmentally nurtured." (Walter Gotshalk, *Art and the Social Order*, University of Chicago Press, 1947, p. 82.) Furthermore, the subjective and objective phases interdepend, complexly, intricately, dialectically.[17]

The seed of creativity is inspiration which flowers and comes to fruition through the mind.

V. Church Nurture of Creativity

Both phases of creativity need nurture. Creativity responds to—yes, is even determined by—the environment. As part of culture, the church should provide that nurture for its musicians. For the Christian artists, the church, as the community of the body of Christ, is (or should be) their base of operations because it is here that they ultimately belong. The church is their cultural home and as guardian, proclaimer, and actuator of those Biblical principles upon which it is founded, the church must not merely tolerate artistic enterprise "out there" but see to it that it nourishes its own artists.

An understanding of creative nurture is necessary if the church is to live out the cultural mandate. The church, concerned with artistic nuture because of the creation and cultural mandates, will make a strong effort to remove the common causes of artistic inertia within its sphere of activity. As a community of believers the church must actively contribute to making the environment conducive to fostering the full use of the creative gift. Certain common blocks will need to be removed.

Complacency on the part of the church body toward music in general and new music in particular is one of the biggest problems the church musician will face. The uninterested, uncaring attitude of many congregations toward originality is well known. Only when the ceaseless round of the expected is sharply broken is there likely to be concern—and only then to insure a return to the comfortable and the familiar. Seldom does a congregation make creativity the norm. The church music program is usually left to itself to develop as is, for when there is no demand and no support for imaginative newness, a barrier is formed environmentally which keeps all but a venturesome few from developing church music programs worthy of the creative example of our Lord. To be satisfied with things as they are, to be complacent about new opportunity, is to provide an atmosphere that stifles the creative gift.

Conformity is another hindrance to creativity. In some ways it is easier to deal with than the uncaring attitude of the complacent, because conformity is active. It demands doing even if the doing is following a prescription. Yet if creativity is anything at all, it is the opposite of conformity by its very definition. Predetermined by other than the artist, formulas and clichés render a music that is dull and repetitive. "To say that a creative artist would not incline to repeat himself exactly is an understatement: he is incapable of it."[18] Thus music composed as a result of forced conformity to the church's dictates in matters of style, taste, harmonic idiom, instrumentation, theological theme, melodic line, or what have you, is composed with the "artist" in a strait jacket and is bound to be a shriveled creativity, if not a contorted, contrived, mechanical, and forced one. It is well known that the church has not only accepted such conformity from mediocre artists but has actively demanded it of many who have endeavored to do better. The result has been a legendary conflict between those artists who (even unknowingly) have taken the creation mandate seriously and the church which purports to stand for truth but in actual practice denies it. Such a rejection of the practical working out of the creation mandate should cause one to pause and consider his stance in the matter. One "cannot dictate to the artist who will illustrate a book what kind of pictures go on which pages [sic]. If what he does is to come alive as art, we must give the artist the freedom to develop through the task set before him."[19]

Rather than demanding conformity, the church should give opportunity to the artist, who, under the influence of the Spirit, creates as a member of the Christian community. By sponsoring and encouraging the composition, performance, and appreciation of music that breaks new ground imaginatively and with integrity, the church testifies in deed to its God-given task of being a beacon of truth in our world.

In addition to removing the blocks of complacency and conformity regarding the artist's work, the church can also help the artistic enterprise by ministering to the personal needs of the artist. As all men do, he has fears, dreams, hopes, pride, failures, inner tensions, conflicting motivations, and so on, which may get in the way of an effective creativity. These personal problems are matters that the church may deal with very successfully, because the gospel of Jesus Christ provides healing, a loving community, and proper goals. The church can provide an essential part of the personal nurture needed by the artist in ministering reconciliation, love, acceptance, and wholeness. The artist needs the church and the church needs the artist.

The church, then, has an active role to play in the fulfillment of the cultural mandate. That it is sorely needed can be seen by society's denial of the doctrine of creation at every turn. We live in an age when mass production dominates even the artistic scene. Our entire culture is permeated by the pop syndrome of stereotype, banality, and cliché, forcefully choking the creativity of our society in general, including that of the church. At stake is the Biblical injunction to be creative.

VI. Summary: Creative Worth and a Church Imperative

We have noted that creation is a matter of forming from the unformed, even as God created order from chaos; the material world is essentially good; God creates not out of compulsion but in freedom; man in freedom has been given a responsibility to create culture; there is an orderly process in creation which is evolutionary rather than revolutionary; man is dependent on God in the objective form-giving of creation and in the subjective intuitive idea stage; God is glorified both in nature and through man's work; creativity needs nurture; and, the essence of creativity is imaginative newness in integrity. Each of these must be acknowledged and acted upon by the church. Whenever man creates that which is trite, banal, unimaginative, or undisciplined, he has denied the doctrine of creation. God's intent is that earthly creativity reflect heavenly creativity.

The church cannot ignore these principles found in the doctrine of creation as it relates to earthly life. Man has been commanded to be a creator, and when he stops creating he stagnates and becomes less than God intended. To be God means to be creative; to be human likewise means to be creative. In bringing both together, the church must establish firmly and unequivocally the directive that all men live out the doctrine of creation in its glorious fullness and splendor.

Through the arts, we both share in God's ongoing work and celebrate the goodness of His work. We are on a pilgrimage—always moving, wrestling, creating. The painful travail of the new must be part of the church music program. The Biblical injunction to "sing a New Song before the Lord, means that it must be new . . . . This requires the ultimate in creativity and therefore the deepest involvement of the most creative elements in our midst."[20] We are being ever called, even in our day, to "sing the praise of God freshly."[21]

We make a fatal mistake, however, in assuming that the church needs new music without qualification. Newness is no guarantee of worth. For example, pop is ever new (the top 40 "hits" change regularly) but its essence is cliché (more on this later). Worthy creative endeavor is the opposite of such traits. To say that music is new is not enough; it must have compositional integrity, creative spark, and craftsmanship, and it must all proceed along a logical evolutionary path. If we believe that God is a painstaking Craftsman in all His works, then

it behooves us as His children to be forever dissatisfied with anything but the best quality that we can produce or encourage our neighbor to produce. If men have been set by God upon the earth to "subdue" and "have dominion over" it, this is also a mandate to learn how to command the best use of all the forms of art.[22]

Knowing that the culture in which we live violates God's intention by pressuring men into emasculating their God-given abilities as makers and appreciators of art, the church music program needs to take active steps to widen and deepen the church's scope of influence in the artistic realm.

The urgent necessity of fully implementing the Biblical idea of creativity is apparent when analyzing the quality of much of our church music. Most of it falls far short of showing the kind of newness, inventiveness, and integrity consistent with the Biblical standard. Many church musicians are more concerned with popular approval, prettiness, novelty, and identification with the standards of the general populace, than in assuming the Biblical pattern of imaginative ongoing creativity.

It is particularly important to note this trend because much of the inferior music being written and disseminated to our churches is labeled "new," as if that were the prime criterion for using it. "New" means nothing if it is not creative (that which breaks new ground *imaginatively* and with *integrity*). Much of the religious "new" is a commercialized variety of afterthought, a warmed-over version of pop music's last frontier, the wake of everchanging fads, a copy of its nonchurch counterpart. Often so-called contemporary religious music has not the slightest relationship to Biblical creativity. Let the church take heed!

Inevitably the question arises: Who is to say that a particular piece of music is creative? If one agrees that standards are a matter of taste and that one taste is as valid as another (hence no "good" or "bad"), then that is the end of it. Carried to its logical conclusion, all music (and everything else for that matter) is of equal value. Such a stance is intolerable for a Christian because it implies that instead of being in a fallen condition all men are perfect, that God has given to every man similar gifts, all used equally well, and that the world is devoid of any value system. Lead then beomes as valuable as gold; any ointment would have served for Mary's anointing the feet of Jesus; the task of providing temple music could have been performed not just by the tribe of Levi, but by any group, trained and ordained or not. The Biblical writers could not have commented on the beauty of a flower, the beauty of the body, or the beauty of holiness, for "beauty" and "ugliness" would be synonymous and the terms would be meaningless. Such a philosophy belongs to the absurdists who deny value, achievement, or authority. It is not a viable option for the Christian.

The search for creativity in a piece of music is the domain of those who have an intuitive *and* knowledgeable grasp of the inner essence of music. Unfortunately there are some musicians who hold Ph.D.'s who show very poor musical taste. They have musical knowledge but no sense of musical rightness. Others have an intuitive sense of worth but cannot explain or articulate the reasons for their conclusions. Both qualities are important for the church musician. He needs the ability to reach right conclusions and the ability to explain to those with whom he works why he feels as he does.

Yet generally, church musicians are able to assess the creative worth of a particular piece of music. Even some of those who are seemingly happy with a consistent diet of "poorish" music give themselves away in unguarded moments by such vernacular expressions as "We are aiming at the 'classics'," or "We do some 'good' things." Granted some musicians will never agree on whether Bach is greater than Beethoven, but there should never be any doubt that J.S. Bach's music has greater musical worth and shows more Biblical creativity than that of Phoebe Knapp. According to the doctrine of creation, music that is maudlin, sentimental, mediocre, and poorly made has no place in church. We not only need a renaissance in the careful choosing of music of integrity and high creativity in our time, *but more importantly, we need the will to use it*—not because of the music, but because the music represents our understanding of all that God has intended us to be and do.

Moreover, the Christian musician, as a man under the creation and cultural mandates, needs to realize the imperative of heeding the Biblical command to be truly creative. This is not a trifling matter that can be dispensed with if he feels like it; nor is it an option to be dropped in favor of something else; there is no choice. To live up to God's intent requires that he take seriously His call to live out life creatively. He cannot turn his back on the full implication of what this means either as a composer, performer, or listener.

Quite frankly, if one were to ask an unbiased observer to name that institution in our society which clearly espouses creativity, we can be sure that he would not name our twentieth-century church. This is an indictment of how we as churchmen feel about the mandate God has given us for being creative. Too often we welcome all kinds of compositional mediocrity into the church and only occasionally give token recognition to music that is solidly crafted upon a sound musical foundation. We do not embrace creativity as a way of life. It is not natural. We do not see it as having much to do with Biblical living, and yet it is there in principle—in the Word. This point cannot be stressed enough. The church is a body which maintains that truth is found in the revealed Word of God. If this body does not practice that which it purports to believe, what kind of credibility does it have? It is encumbent upon those who believe that the Bible expresses God's intention for man to live up to those intentions. God our Father, the Creator, did not make us to be artistically lethargic, insensitive, indolent, or animal-like. He gave us a job to do—to subdue or develop the potential of His gift of a world which, though far from perfect, is still His creation. We cannot in any way escape this mandate. It is ours. The question is: What are we the church going to do with it?

The church fulfills the creative and cultural mandates as it becomes a microcosm of true creativity. Church music, as an expression of the church's life should be a vital force in affirming that the church stands for integrity, wholeness, and creativity. The doctrine of creation as exhibited in church music can show people how to live bountifully amidst the wealth of inspired idea and well-made form. The church must testify to the world through nurture, use, and attitude, that creativity is both a responsibility and a gift from God the Father, Maker of heaven and earth.

3

THE *IMAGO DEI*

I. The Broad *Imago Dei*

The doctrine of the *imago Dei* is closely tied to that of creation and is necessary here for a fuller understanding of man's nature as it relates to artistic activity, both without and especially within the church. It is a doctrine which consists of a multitudinous array of statements and counterstatements. Theologians historically have had a difficult time arriving at its meaning. An interpretation of the Biblical material in two aspects of the doctrine's many ramifications will be our purpose here, and will serve to illuminate and heighten important musical considerations for a pastoral ministry of music.

Some of the more common interpretations of the doctrine are: man has been made in the bodily image of God; the *imago Dei* is centered around man's personhood; man's capacity for right and wrong, his moral sense, is the *imago Dei*; man is made in the image of God as he enters into a right relationship with God through Jesus Christ; the *imago* is to be found in God-given freedom and responsibility; man's reason constitutes the image; man has been given dominion over the world, and so forth. All of these views undoubtedly have some validity, though our perusal of the doctrine will take us far afield from most of these analyses to a somewhat less familiar, yet fertile ground.

The last one above, dominion-having, needs special explanation. We have made much about the creation mandate in the last chapter, saying that it is a God-given obligation for man to develop the potential of the world by subduing the earth, or having dominion over it, even in terms of culture in general and art in particular. Some theologians have felt that the *imago Dei* is to be found in man's having dominion over the earth and in fulfilling the creation mandate. However, lest there be confusion in understanding our thesis which is quite different from this, we must note here that the *imago Dei* is not identical with the creation mandate. The creation mandate can only be accomplished because of man's being made in the image of God. They are not the same thing. The two, the *imago Dei* and the creation mandate, are separate. Several authors have made this observation. One notes that "this dominion over the animals [the creation mandate] is not in itself the *imago Dei,* but is the first opportunity for the image to be exercised in a definite way."[1] Another says that the dominion of the earth "should not be equated with the fact that he [man] has been created in the image of God— although this mistake is often made—but it should be conceived as its consequence."[2] The *imago Dei* is concerned with man's inner nature, the creation mandate with a command for continuing creation. Fulfillment of the mandate is achieved because we are equipped to do so through God's gift of the *imago Dei*. The former comes through the latter.

There are two aspects to the doctrine of the *imago Dei*. The first is a broad one in which all men participate; the second, a more narrow view, applies only to redeemed men. Though some theologians adopt one side or the other, most agree that both are necessary if the full truth of the doctrine is to be known.

The first, the broad aspect of the *imago Dei,* was formulated in order to emphasize the fact that man, made in the image of God, did not completely lose the image in the Fall. He did not become a devil when he fell into sin. Not that he retained his Godly inheritance without blemish, for if we could have observed man in his original perfection, we would by comparison agree with Calvin's perspective that what remained of the *imago* after the Fall is but a "horrible deformity." Yet the image, though tarnished and imperfect, is nonetheless still there. Even after the Fall, man is made in God's image.

Of the many ways in which theologians have described the *imago* within the broad view, one is particularly important for the church musician, namely, creativity. We have said that God by His very nature is Creator, and a valid, if not the best, adjective to describe Him is "creative," since His very essence continually creates and recreates. It would be inconceivable to have such a God create a being in His own image and not find that creature bodying forth in his very nature that particular quality which is of God's essence.

> We are told in Genesis 1:26 that the Creator proposes to make man in His own "image and likeness." There has been much speculation about what might be the meaning or content of this likeness. On the basis of the text itself, we may observe that up to this point in the narrative, the reader has been told only one thing about God that would enable him to attach some content to the notion of likeness to God. He has been told of God's activity as the Creator. One might therefore justly conclude that the meaning of the image and likeness—or at least one meaning of it—is that man shall be *like God in his creativity*. Be creative as your Father in heaven is creative.[3]

Dorothy Sayers, noting that the writer of Genesis has written only of God's creative activity up to the statement, "So God created man in His own image, in the image of God created He him" (Genesis 1:27, KJV) says:

> But had the author of *Genesis* anything particular in his mind when he wrote? It is observable that in the passage leading up to the statement about man, he has given no detailed information about God. Looking at man, he sees in him something essentially divine, but when we turn back to see what he says about the original upon which the "image" of God was molded, we find only the single assertion, "God created." The characteristic common to God and man is apparently that: the desire and the ability to make things.[4]

Classical Christian thinkers such as Augustine, Bonaventure, and Aquinas, regardless of other differences, all agree that the *imago* can be seen as man's creativity. He is intended by God to be creative in his very bones, for the creative force is deeply ingrained in his nature; it is the core of his being.

There can be no doubt. He is created in the image of the Creator, and his ability to create and shape the world is his only because he has received it in the *imago Dei*.

The creativity given to man in the *imago Dei* is an endowment given to all men. Not everyone is a Bach or a Beethoven but all participate in the creative gift. The notion that creativity is the possession of only a few is repudiated by the broad sense of the *imago Dei*. Every man is to live bountifully, which is to say, creatively. Actually, many of the various ways of explaining that man is made in the image of God in the broad sense can be seen in this single idea. To be a creator requires reason, freedom, responsibility, natural rightness, love toward that which is being created, personality, and a predilection for what is beyond oneself. The *imago* is literally man's endowment for creativity in a very large sense, involving much more than we normally associate with it. It is a mark of his humanity and applies to all men in every area of life, regardless of his being a saint or a sinner, regenerate or unregenerate.

Everyone, then, has rooted in the depths of his being creative forces that indicate a special relationship or correspondence to God and that form the basis of his creaturely existence. Living creatively is much more than artistic activity. It is living all of life in such a manner that we fulfill the potential of our humanity. In a sense, one's own life can become a work of art as we exercise our gifts responsibly in freedom. The mundane and ordinary things of life both relationally and environmentally can be materials for becoming and making what is not.

Great artists, however, have unique gifts and can show to us in particularly clear ways the creative meaning of the *imago Dei*. Emmanuel Chapman notes that "in a certain manner art may be said to be the highest natural likeness of the activity of God."[5] The artist makes visible in concrete form that which others do not readily see. He apprehends relationships where none appear to exist and sees potential in the most ordinary and unlikely things. The artist's making is free, unforced, and within the art form itself, inherently purposeful. He incarnates pure idea into powerful form in such a way that the resulting beauty is approachable, apprehensible, and correspondent in some degree to every man's natural, God-given sensitivity to beauty. His works are not purely utilitarian. The reason for creating is not what he can make the object do for him; rather, as an expression of man's creative nature, art's reason for being is the pure joy it brings in being beautiful and true. The artist wrestles and overcomes the material of the world so that something unique is brought into being. This doing of something new, this ability to be original, to overcome the confusion and chaos of the world, to see and hear where others know only a void, to bring joy through beauty and truth, is the closest he can come (within the broad view) to fully apprehending his having been made in the creative image of God.

The fact that man has a creative nature that can soar to great creative heights does not mean that his creativity will always take a wholesome direction. Sloth, indifference, selfishness, pride, or any number of similar things can rob and warp his creativity so as to produce the trivial, the mediocre, or the grotesque.

Because of man's disobedience, his creating is a fallen one, and though it remains as part of his glorious heritage, it is man's destiny to struggle continuously against the heaviness of the world so as to turn that creativity into worthy channels. Every man must contend with a fallen condition. He will always be creative (in the general sense, not in our usage of the term) in some way, for that is his nature—that will not stop. The problem is to use that creativity as God intended he should—a creativity that is the glory of man because it is worthy of his Maker.

Man, then, is made in the image of God (in the broad sense) by virtue of the fact that he has God-given creative abilities. He corresponds to God in his creativity. That which he makes, however, shows him to be a creator who is far from perfect, but who has the capacity of reaching toward perfection in his making. All men have been given creative gifts and those gifts which are *creatively* (breaking new ground imaginatively and with integrity) exercised show the *imago* with particular lucidity.

Church music is affected by the broad *imago Dei* in that the arts are part of man's general activity even before they are a part of the activity of the redeemed. Churchmen are first men and they display the broad sense of the *imago* in all their activities—including those of church music. There is much musical activity in churches, for all men participate in the gift, yet in looking at the activity and the product of the activity, one wonders just how true a picture is being painted by the church of man's being made in the creative image of God! Every year thousands of pieces of music are published, disseminated, and performed which speak more of man's self-indulgence than man's birthright. Wherever it is found, all musical degradation (poor music) says explicitly that man made in God's image is less than his humanity calls him to be. Church music that does not clearly exhibit a genuine creativity has no place in church music because it defiles the *imago Dei.*

A viable church music program cannot be built if this doctrine is ignored. The musician as a truly creative artist clearly proclaims that God made mankind in His image—in the image of the Creator. One's program must be a collective declaration that the Creator God begat a creator man.

II. The Narrow *Imago Dei*

The narrow view of the *imago Dei* holds that the image was destroyed in the Fall; that man, having come into sin, no longer retains any vestige of his former stature. Only as he is redeemed, as he comes to God through Jesus Christ, the perfect image, is the *imago* restored. The image cannot be known outside of a saving relationship with God.

This view of the *imago Dei* should be understood on three levels: (1) man is *in* the image of God; (2) he is *becoming* the image of God; and (3) he *images* God. First, man is in the image of God as he accepts the propitiatory work of Christ. Through the atonement, his debt has been paid and he stands before his Maker justified, perfect in righteousness. The *imago Dei* on this level, then, is viewed through Jesus Christ and shows man to be made in God's image, complete, and without blemish. This is how God looks at redeemed man.

The second way of looking at the *imago* is in man's *becoming* the image of God, or to put it another way, his being conformed to the image of the Son. Here the Christian life is a process of growing into Christ's likeness. His suffering, trials and tribulations, testings of faith, learning to love more fully, grappling with creative expression, and so on are a necessary polishing and refining of self so that the image in him comes to resemble more clearly the Creator and Redeemer. The rough edges, the flaws in one's character, the hidden secrets of the heart, the warring of the "old man," the indulgence into selfishness and pride, the setting up of idols, all must be surrendered and overcome. As he slowly moves toward what God would have him be, he becomes more and more like Christ, the perfect Image. The individual Christian, then, views his own pilgrimage as a growth process realizing that the image grows stronger and brighter the closer one comes to the Source. He sees himself as a "becomer" reaching out for the perfect *image.*

The third way of viewing the *imago Dei* is to understand the word *image* more as an active verb than passive noun. Man *images* God. He shows God outwardly to the world. To image God is to shine as a beacon on a hill so that all might see and hear God in us. Berkouwer says:

> being like God can shine forth as a light in the world. It is the light of good works: let *your* light shine among the people so that they may *observe* your lofty actions and give glory to your heavenly Father (Matt. 5:16).[6]

Man tells about God as others watch his actions. To "image" is to make visible, to represent God in deed in such a manner that the meaning behind the action is seen. The *imago Dei* is a "summons to action; a challenge to conduct, a guide to behaviour."[7] Man in the narrow sense of the image is to show forth an imitation of Christ in the highest and best sense.

The restoration of the narrow *imago* calls us to a level of faith commitment in which obedience and responsibility to the full implications of the Word are paramount. In Christ we belong in community, and we are responsible to God not only for ourselves, but also for our neighbor. The attitude that we must care for the world is deeply ingrained in the Christian religion. We set ourselves right with God in order to serve both Him and our fellow man. The narrow image of God is not inwardly static, but rather, outwardly dynamic. The image is nothing if it is not an active representation of God as we serve Him with the gifts He has given us.

> But the actual image is found in the *use* of these created qualities in active and dynamic service of God. Thus and only thus can man reflect God, mirror God, be in God's image. The image of God does not consist of qualities in themselves, but in created man's life *in actu,* in action, and in functioning.[8]

The image must be a representation of God here on earth while man is in loving relationship with the Creator, serving Him.

Imaging God cannot be accomplished by the Christian who becomes a mystic or ascetic, withdrawn and hidden away from the world. Representation of God cannot be representation until there is someone on the receiving end. We cannot image God in a vacuum and merely sit back in isolation waiting to go to heaven. As Christians we are to see the world as a grand opportunity for witness, for showing forth the *imago,* and for imaging our "being-like-God." We welcome the world rather than withdraw from it so that we can witness to the full meaning of the image of God in man. The new birth makes us new creatures who are called, commissioned, and commanded to glorify our Creator. We fulfill God's intent and purpose to glorify Him as we are *in* the image, as we *become* more like the image, and as we *image* the image.

The imaging of the redeemed is articulated in every sphere of life: economic, social, political, domestic, religious, and aesthetic. It is a Christian's witness through and to all areas of culture that gives us the best idea of the breadth and depth of his witness. It is not a matter of talking, of verbal barrages; it is expression of God's intention through *what we do.* Redeemed imaging, pure and simple, is good action consistent with the Word. It shows the very core of what we really are, rather than what we say we are, and this is the proof of our confession, our witness to all of our culture. Nothing is exempt. What we read, how we spend our money, the care for our families, the intensity of our study, where we go, the help we give our neighbor, our consistency in church attendance, the music we listen to, the television programs we watch, and the language we use, are only a few examples of ways that our imaging impacts the world.

We have made the assertion that the broad view of the *imago* can best be explained by the all-inclusive use of the term *creativity.* We, by virtue of being men, have a creative nature. The Fall has tarnished our creativity, yet as creatures made in God's image, we can ever rise to new heights of creative activity.

Redemption affects man's general creativity. In a well-known passage taken from various writings of Nicolas Berdyaev, W. Paul Jones says,

> Man is created in the *imago Dei*; this image and likeness is restored to him through the redemptive activity of Jesus Christ. Here is the key to the Christian understanding: The God in whose image man has been formed and to which he has been restored is the creator God. Therefore, redeemed life, life in the Spirit, *is* the life of creativity. Redemption in itself is negative; it means liberation *from*. Consequently, the intent of redemption, its positive corollary, is liberation *for* creativity.[9]

One must see, then, in the narrow view of the *imago Dei,* an intensification of man's general creative powers because he now has a direct link through Jesus Christ to the source of all creativity.

More specifically, artistic creativity should be expected to be heightened by one's becoming a Christian. One is not to turn one's back on good creative action (breaking new ground imaginatively and with integrity) though it is unfortunately true that much so-called "Christian art" is inferior. A Christian needs to demonstrate that he is made in the image of his Creator because he now represents Him in a much higher sense. He images God even through his attitude toward art. Edith Schaeffer comes right to the point in saying:

It is true that all men are created in the image of God, but Christians are supposed to be *conscious* of that fact, and being conscious of it should recognize the importance of living artistically, aesthetically, and creatively, as creative creatures of the Creator.[10]

And again she says:

In other words, are we, who have been made in the image of our Creator, and who acknowledge and understand what that means because we know God exists, and experience communication with Him—are we to be less creative than those who do not know that the Creator made them in His image, and who have no contact with Him?[11]

It is easier to ask the question than to actually increase creativity. Yet the arts should be one of the highest manifestations of the creative gift. Therefore we should expect redeemed man made in God's image to reflect God's great creativity in his own creativity. Yet experience has shown us that often Christians stay on the same banal artistic plateau, making, appreciating, and performing works of "art" which are so poor that a mockery is made of God-given creativity. A tainted *imago Dei* results.

Redeemed imaging is a much more potent, personal, and specific type of imaging than that found in the broad image. To show forth God's glory in terms of one's actions is no small matter for the Christian. This is a matter of witnessing and testifying to the one concrete reality that has made all the difference in the world and in the individual. It cannot be taken lightly or as an option. What a Christian does, whether he wishes it so or not, shows the world his concept of God.

III. Summary: Musical Imaging

We have said that in the creation mandate, man, as man, is given the responsibility to aid in God's continuing creation. In the broad sense of the *imago Dei,* he is endowed with the tools for this task and creates because it is part of his nature. Now in the narrow sense of the *imago Dei* he faces the prospect that through his actions (i.e., music) *God is shown* in a very definite way. Church music is testimony, and the church is a place where believers worship corporately, utilizing cultural expressions to show what God has done, what He means, and what He is.

In the discussion of the broad view we noted that because of the Fall the creativity of man was ultimately weakened. In spite of that fact and in response to the urge to make things, man has created great and noble works that glorify the Creator. The narrow view states that the image is a redeemed relationship with God through Jesus Christ. This relationship has the potential to restore man to a fuller creative capacity. The Christian has an active part to play in this restoration as formerly noted when he (1) *is in* (the new birth) the image, (2) *becomes like* the image, and (3) *images* the *imago Dei.*

But it is one of the scandals of so-called Christian society that regenerate man often feels such little complusion to fulfill the creative potential. What we have said about the need for true creativity in unregenerate man in the broad *imago* must be multiplied "seventy times seven" for Christians, who in addition to the broad image also participate in the narrow image. The Christian who refuses to rise above vulgarity, mediocrity, and even the good (as opposed to the best) in the arts is exhibiting a distorted, warped, twisted, even mutilated version of the image of God.

If this were not bad enough! The church musician must also contend with the listless discrimination shown the general public by many religious periodicals, music publishing firms, music seminars, and Christian radio and television programs. For example, record reviewers seldom criticize a recording for poor quality of musical composition. It seems that unreasoned bias and blind obeisance are replacing careful evaluation and sound thinking. Conversation about the contemporary church music dilemma " . . . has too often gotten down to the level of a shouting match between the purists who hold that old is good, and the faddists who feel that the latest is the greatest."[12] The cyclical spiral of musical mediocrity is perpetuated by endless publishing of "music that sells," seminars for the general but uninformed Christian music lover held by "prestigious" musicians with commercial musical standards, and the Madison Avenue approach to selling the religious experience of many newly converted singing stars with little or no concern for the inherent quality of the music used in the testimony.

Ironically, many of the radio and television programs that purport to witness to the fullness of God's bounteous riches, miss the mark when it comes to music. Such riches are supposed to be appropriated in everyday living, spiritually, psychologically, and physically, for they are riches set in a sumptuous banquet-feast for all those in the narrow *imago Dei*. And while many of these radio and television programs often have the very best in the way of equipment, studio buildings, and staff expertise, the *imago Dei,* the redeemed imaging as it is shown in the general quality of the musical compositions aired from day to day, is often one of emaciated privation, an *imago Dei* gaunt and hollow, a malnourished, spindly, feeble creativity in contradistinction to the abundance of God's gifts advanced in the verbalized sermons, teachings, and discussions.

These few examples of the religious musical culture that often confront the new Christian are overwhelmingly strong in their influence. When we realize that the God-given creative potential in the redeemed image is largely cast aside, one cringes at the monstrous musical-theological hoax being perpetrated on the religious world. It is monstrous not only in size but in quality because the Christian in this situation images God in terms of musical poverty and degradation, quite incongruous with what he knows or is being taught of the almighty Creator.

God the Creator as shown forth by the church musician's music is often a frightening prospect! We image God in the music we do. When the program is hit-or-miss, we show forth a God who lacks purpose and direction; when our work is not well prepared, we image a God who is lazy and slothful; when performance preparation is a last minute affair, we show forth a procrastinating God; when our performance of music lacks vitality or artistic grace, we show God to be inert; when our musical choices revolve around our favorite style or body of composition, God is seen as rigid and unbending; and, above all, when the music we choose lacks creativity in the full sense, we image forth a God of "creative" mediocrity. The church musician must take note, for there is no getting around the fact that our actions speak louder than our words.

They who experience what is believed about the narrow *imago Dei* and are therefore His disciples are responsible to, and in fact do, image God. The question each church musician faces is not, "Shall I?" but, "What will be the image set forth?" To be made in God's image once and then reformed into His image through Christ is to have now an evangelistic reason for setting forth in music a higher and more noble image than that found in the broad image. Man may be made in God's image in general, but the Christian specifically images God as Creator and Redeemer in all of His glory. Redeemed imaging is the *imago Dei* at its highest and best. We cannot afford to let it be anything less.

The church musician, then, is responsible for music that sets forth the *imago Dei* to the world. In this way he is showing care for his neighbor and is fulfilling the great commission. This imaging can only be carried out when his music exhibits creativity, integrity and care in performance, for the *imago Dei* is shown through the notes.

4

THE INCARNATION

I. Divine and Artistic Incarnation

The incarnation of the Son of God is the main event in God's disclosure of Himself to mankind. The Son was at the same time fully God and fully man, neither nature compromised because of the other. Although He was divine and human, Jesus was untainted by sin. The act of His infleshment was accomplished through His own free and sovereign will and was motivated by the desire to call us to Himself in divine love. His becoming the God-man to mediate between God and us is indeed the supreme example of that love.

The initiative God took in making a way for us to be reconciled unto Himself shows the Eternal united with the temporal, Spirit with matter, the Word in flesh—Jesus, the material form of God Almighty. The incarnation was the Divine entering the stream of history in a physical way, thus refuting the notion that the temporal is inherently evil, the spiritual good, and each is forever limited to going separate if not opposite ways.

> In Christ, the infinite chasm between God and man was permanently traversed. This means no more division between sacred and secular acts. . . . The sacred entered the profane, ending the eternal duality of the Greeks.[1]

It was Christ's being a man in the world, being with us in a tangible way, that vividly portrayed His immanence. God is present in various degrees and levels within creation and the fact that He came in the flesh gives us assurance and comfort that He did not forsake what He created. In Christ, we know and feel that He is with us. He knows our joys, sorrows, failings, weaknesses, and sinfulness, yet He loved us and freely pardoned our sin. He is a God who is here and who cares. Not that He becomes identical with us, for a radical immanence in which the distinction between God and us is eroded by an unhealthy familiarity is just as erroneous as a radical transcendence in which God is banished to the heavens, out of touch with the world and out of touch with the day-to-day events of our lives. Both are needed, but in the incarnation exists the ultimate, supreme, and final step in showing to us that God cares deeply for His creation.

Art itself is incarnational. The artist takes the material of the earth and through the creative process causes it to flesh out his intent. That which did not exist materially becomes available for man's apprehension. Idea takes upon itself real form. Thought is embodied by matter. The "word," as it were, becomes "flesh." Essentially, then, an artist is best seen as an incarnator, for he deals in concrete realities, is earthy in his method of sharing his vision, and has purpose in what he creates. The church musician participates in the fleshing out process not only as he composes but also as he re-creates musical works with various ensembles. That is, music as it is in score form, though having material configuration, really takes shape only when it is performed. The process of performing, then, is also incarnational.

II. Pastoral Humility

The doctrine of the incarnation is highly instructive for two important areas in the ministry of music. The first has to do with the pastoral stance of the church musician, and the second with communication. "In becoming man, God humbled Himself" is a statement so profound that it is next to impossible for man to grasp its meaning. The infinite God became finite man. As Richard Crashaw has said,

> Welcome all wonders in one sight,
> Eternity shut in a span,
> Summer in winter, day in night,
> Heav'n in earth, and God in man!
> Great little One! Whose glorious Birth
> Lifts earth to heav'n, stoops heav'n to earth.[2]

Christ, stripped of His glory, condescended to become human flesh, emptying Himself of His power, place, and authority. He became the lowest among men for our sakes. He experienced the disrepute of finally being deserted by His adoring and cheering multitudes, and was left with only a handful of disheartened and bewildered disciples. He endured humiliation, shame, bodily and mental suffering, was accused unjustly, and finally died a disgraceful and painful death. Jesus was a man who gave up everything to become a servant to those who by natural right should have been His subjects. The tenor of the entire Christ-event was a humble service illustrated in capsule form by Jesus' washing the disciples' feet. This act was merely no

> isolated object lesson. It was a drama expressing the total character of Jesus' mission. He stripped Himself of power and privilege. He poured Himself out in the service of mankind. He purged the deepest recesses of the human spirit.[3]

Jesus, in His humility, was indisputably, as Bonhoeffer puts it, a "man existing for others." He showed no pretentiousness, no snobbery, no exclusiveness. He kept company with prostitutes and tax collectors as well as with teachers and rabbinical scholars. He turned none away and treated those who came to Him with kindness, gentleness, and a patient endurance. Jesus, the Christ, the Son of God, became a servant.

Christ expects His followers to exhibit His humility. He taught this principle to His disciples. Using Himself as a model, He said:

> Ye call me Master and Lord: and ye say well; for so I am. If I then, your Lord and Master, have washed your feet; ye also ought to wash one another's feet.

For I have given you an example, that ye should do as I have done to you (John 13:13-15 KJV).

The Christian is not excused from humble service. He is to endure pain, suffering, and hardship on behalf of those to whom he is called. Every Christian (especially the music director) is to emulate the suffering servant image which is revealed in Old Testament literature and which culminates in Jesus Christ.

Humility for the church musician is necessary because in the course of working with his congregation he is often called upon (to a greater degree than any other minister) to give up things even as our Lord did, things which are meaningful, necessary, and sometimes which form the very heart of his artistic vision. Inevitably he is better trained in music than his parishioners, having a more refined intuitive sense, a broader and deeper knowledge, and greater experience. Musically speaking he exists on an exalted level, while the congregation is considerably below him. A situation in which the musician chooses music out of his own musical understanding, while considering the congregation to be beneath his musical dignity, is sure to polarize the two. The musician feels that he cannot give up what he knows to be right and the congregation does not grasp what he is trying to do. It is not that he lacks good intentions. In his effort to promote good music which speaks well of the gospel, he works very hard. He is a tireless promoter, conductor, educator, and scholar. His music program attempts to be a model of Christian artistic endeavor. But the danger is that eventually musical pride, undetected at first and hidden under good intentions, will come to play a greater part in the musician's personality so that the classic breach between congregation and musician inevitably opens. The musician will feel that the congregation knows nothing and should say nothing about the music, and the congregation will feel that the musician is an arrogant elitist who uses them for his own musical gratification. It is here that the doctrine of the incarnation can bring healing to a painful split—a split that only gets worse as basic positions harden on both sides.

The church is a body; it cannot exist without a sense of togetherness between musician, pastor, and people. It is vital that the music director view amateur musical expression through the incarnation. One cannot have congregational togetherness without participation and there is no participation if music exists on a consistently higher level than people's ability for comprehension. The Lord, in coming to earth, came not to the elite only, but to all people. In following Christ's example, the pastoral musician must swallow his musical pride and take into consideration (without condescension) others who are less artistically advanced. The opinions, tastes, and suggestions of those who know less than the minister of music will not be cast aside. Only as a church music program begins to take seriously the views of the less skillful can it be considered incarnational. The minister of music must stoop in humility.

The doctrine of the incarnation demands that the musician become a pastor. When the primary concern is for the music itself, the pastoral role of care for people will be minimal. Such an emphasis does not do justice to the theology of the incarnation for it often puts the musically poor, desolate, and drunken (musically speaking) on a lower plane than he who "serves." As a servant the music director is to wash humanity's feet, to minister to people where they are—not to lament the possibility of having to lower his station in life.

The Christian message does not just fit in with a particular cultural situation. As the musician is attuned to the local church in which he finds himself, he will embrace with great joy the incarnational approach to music-making. He should become one with his people by lowering himself artistically if necessary or, perchance, by raising his personal standards if circumstances warrant. Then, he can have a point of contact with them—a demonstration of his pastoral love. The Christian community, as Calvin Seerveld points out, is in desperate need of leaders such as scholars, artists, and writers who stay close to and form a bond with those who are usually less proficient in cultural matters. If the cultural mandate is to be fulfilled by the church, its leaders (including the musicians) must not exhibit an intellectualism that will alienate those whom they serve.[4] Concern for music has its place, but in the pastoral ministry of music, concern for people will come first. It is important that we have

> competent musicians with a pastoral orientation. Leadership from the aristocratic stance is the result of convictions about musical standards (and this must be neither despised nor lost); leadership from the pastoral stance is the result of love, which seeks to enable the people to perform their liturgy. As in all forms of Christian service, the servant form is the model.[5]

The church musician, then, shows the humility exhibited by God Himself in the incarnation. He is to become one with his people no matter what their cultural state; the concern shown through his musical program is a concern for the congregation first, rather than concern for his personal artistic standards. In his role as a pastoral musician he must be willing to set aside pride and minister to people where they are by showing the love of God through his musical infleshment of the mystery of the incarnation. He has no time to mourn his lack of position, the disrespect shown his professional abilities, or the unfairness of people who are musically inferior but who dictate his course. As does every other Christian, he needs to show God's love. His basic philosophical stance and the premise from which his entire program comes must be predicated upon this position. In servant form, the pastoral duty of the musican is to care, to be concerned, to show regard for—in a word, to love.

Without detracting from what we have just said, it would be beneficial to pause a moment to reflect on the word *love*. From the foregoing, one might be tempted to conclude erroneously that pastoral love means "doing what the people want." Authentic love, though, is much more than this. Pain and suffering may not look like the love of God now. Denying a child the pleasure of consuming an entire box of chocolate candies does not look like love to the child at the time. Love goes beyond what is immediately apparent.

It does not mean catering to and fulfilling every fleeting whim. Authentic love is responsible and takes into account final well-being.

III. Communication, Relevance, and Content

Every congregation has its own idea about what music is best suited for worship. Without being an uncritical "yes-man," the incarnational approach to directing the church music program means that the musician must be responsive to the congregation's thinking, realizing that church music must have significant meaning for them. He must take into account their musical profile. Music which, over the long haul, is completely incomprehensible, even baffling, cannot serve the needs of worship. Music must be intelligible and yet not be entertainment. Indeed,

> we disobey Him if what we do and sing and say and pray is unintelligible to those who come, or to whom we go. We further disobey this command if we dress up the truths of the Gospel so that they appeal only in a romantic light— so that the death of Jesus gains a "kind of gloss it didn't have." The irrelevancy of Christianity, as it appears to many, lies partly in our inability to communicate, and also partly because what we communicate is only part of the truth, or a dressed up version of it.
> Basically the problem is one of communication. [6]

We have discussed the incarnation in the light of the musician's need for a pastoral stance of humility. Also, we have seen that our concern for people must supersede our concern for music. But the doctrine is also highly instructive for communication methodology. On the one hand, we must communicate from a common base of understanding; and on the other, our communication should say what we intend. The facts of the communication must not be distorted by the mode of communication.

Both the incarnation and art can be viewed as communication methods. Speaking theologically, man did not go to God. It was God who established the relationship that man could not build himself. Man brings nothing to the covenant. God accepts him as he is, in sin and degradation. In coming to man, God came in terms people could understand. It is, as it were, a translation of God into meaningful language. He who dwells in light unapproachable, who is larger than the meanings of man's words and symbols, and who cannot be known as God, comes as a man on man's own terms, and in a form that man can apprehend. God as man, then, is no longer incomprehensible. He is unmistakably relevant.

The theme of relevancy is one that has been taken up in full force by the contemporary church. Terms such as "identify with," "here and now," "meet the people where they are," and "all things to all men" (often made into a travesty of Paul's original intent) are everyday jargon. "God took on human flesh, now let us not be afraid to incarnate the gospel further into whatever form necessary to get the message across." In our present society of mass culture, many believe that the gospel should affirm the forms of that culture so that through these relevant forms, mass man might be able to see and hear in his own language. The church has no more important task than communicating the gospel to men, which means in no uncertain terms that the church must speak so that it can be understood. Knowledge precedes faith, and only as we speak intelligibly can knowledge be communicated. The church, figuratively speaking, needs to get out of the nave and chancel and into the street. It must speak on the level of the addressee.

Yet more needs to be said about relevance. Note the following quote, which shows how relevancy, if brought to its ultimate conclusion, can go far astray from its intended purpose.

> "What is it you do exactly?"
> "I'll order a bingo first, if you don't mind."
> "Long as it's not on my tab."
> The reverend shook his hands. "I have an arrangement with the management. Free bingo." He signaled a chromeplated waitress. When his drink arrived the reverend added, "I don't suppose you'd care to be converted."
> "Right. Is that what you do?"
> "Originally," said Rev. Cockspur. He tossed down his greenish liquor. "I came out to Esperanza three years ago, sent by my religious association to convert young people. I selected the Fringe to begin, to start bringing them under the wing." He waved for another drink. "Wish I had a little balsam, enough to let me get my daddles on a journey."
> "You take drugs, too?"
> The reverend frowned into his fresh drink. "Initially I realized I wouldn't have a chance of reaching the young people of the Fringe unless I learned their ways, otherwise they'd write me off as just another joskin. First I picked up on their way of talking, after which I acquired their drinking habits. It brought me much closer to them. To press even nearer I started joining the kids on drug experiences. So now I've reached a position where I can really communicate with them and I'm an alcoholic, a drug addict, a prescription drug fiend and I'm living with two albino nymphomaniacs in a third floor ghetto down the street."[7]

Obviously there is more to communication than just relevance. We must speak in a language understood by people, but we must also be faithful to the content of the message. The form of the communication is not everything. It is when the two, form and content, are in conflict that we have problems. We must be relevant in order to communicate, but our relevancy must be under the judgment of the gospel message.

It is instructive to note that Jesus, in taking upon Himself the form of a man, remained sinless. He found it possible to be relevant without participating in the activities of the dishonest tax collectors, prostitutes, and thieves. Relevance is important, but it does not mean the wholesale assent to a way of life which is diametrically opposed to all that the gospel stands for. It would indeed be wrong to equate moral ineptitude with poor music of some sort, thus concluding that even as one can sin morally, one can sin musically, and because Jesus did not sin morally, the church musician ought not to sin musically. Such reasoning is indeed faulty and ludicrous. There is a more advantageous way of coming to grips with the problem of relevance and communication as it relates to music in the church.

We have said that knowledge precedes faith (i.e., if one is to believe, he must believe in something, and until he knows about the atoning work of Christ he cannot believe). The only possible way that this type of knowledge can be given is through verbalized statements. Language, being the best specific meaning-symbolization system man has, is the only way that the facts of the atonement can be given. Church music (speaking of words and music separately) cannot challenge language at this point. Explicit meanings are outside the realm of music; hence music in the church does not need to concern itself with giving propositional information. The direct witness of the gospel is the domain of language—even in a song.

Musical relevance, then, cannot be considered on a par with verbal relevance. Understanding language and understanding music are on two completely different levels. Verbal understanding is specific understanding (as specific as language can get), while musical understanding is less specific. It is possible to answer the question "Do you understand?" regarding a propostional statement, but to answer the same question about a piece of music is to plunge into a tremendously murky area where rational understanding may take many directions. Relevance insofar as it promotes the specific facts of the gospel is by far more important to language than to music. Relevance in musical terms is much more akin to general familiarity than to a finely honed understanding. Musical relevance, then, does not have to bear the responsibility for the rational understanding of the literal Word, because that is the domain of language. This is not to say that musical relevance is unimportant. It is important, but it should operate on a less intense plane than we have hitherto assumed.

Relevancy, if carried to the extreme, would be the death of a prophetic music ministry, because musical life would depend on what is and not on what should be. The peculiar twists and turns of mass culture, which is largely anti-Christian in its orientation, would entirely determine the music of a church. The incarnation did show that God stooped to earth. He did lower Himself and become man. He did become relevant. *But Christ stooped in order that He might pick man up.* There is no way in which the incarnation can be seen as an excuse for a life of musical deprivation and total cultural determinism. Just the opposite is true. The incarnation is the gate that opens to the whole man God's endless, boundless, and unfathomable creative energy through life in Christ.

Communication is commonly thought of as a process which takes place when one imposes his views on another. This idea is akin to propaganda. Communication thus becomes pressing on people what they do not have, making the technique parallel to the Madison Avenue concept of selling something. There is often great frustration on both sides. The communicator is frustrated because what he is trying to say is not "getting across," and the one receiving the communication is frustrated because he may not like the content of the message, or he does not understand it, or he does not like the "package" it is in. He feels that he is being exploited and treated as a thing, for exploitation is the essence of communication as propaganda. Propagandizing the gospel perverts it. Jesus' communication was implicit. It involved discovery, relationship, and dialogue; there were no high-powered selling techniques, sales gimmicks, or slogans. The truth of God does not lend itself to brainwashing, and if such browbeating takes place, the message is inevitably changed. To propagandize something whose content resists imposition can only result in the distortion of that which is communicated. The gospel is not a candidate for the hard sell.

Consequently, we are forced to conclude that communication methodology is vitally important. If the message given is to be the message that was actually intended, we must see to it (as best we can) that both message and method are "agreeable" with each other. And the incarnation is highly instructive as a model for that unification.

The incarnation can be seen as the perfect work of art in the sense that there is an insoluble unity between what Christ had to say and the way He said it. The form and the content supported each other. That is, His life and actions (form) corresponded to what He was and to what He said (content). There was the highest fusion between the two because the content and the form, though separate, were not separated. Indeed, they could not have been. There was an organic relationship in which one without the other would have destroyed or at least distorted the whole. G. William Jones is very persuasive on this matter:

> The question of content, or of what the work communicates to its beholder, is actually inseparable from the consideration of the question of form, or of how the work is constructed . . . what a work has to communicate and how it communicates it are one and the same thing . . . consider a poorly executed film production in which the producers are concerned only with presenting their message visually and care little about camera placement and movement, lighting, the technical quality of sound recording, and editing . . . the form of their presentation has not only influenced negatively their intended message, but has actually been part of the content [a negative content] conveyed to the viewer. This perhaps serves to illustrate the mistake of those who endeavor, consciously or not, to separate content from form.[8]

It is very possible that our method of expressing truth can negate the truth we have to set forth. According to the incarnation one cannot divorce what one says from how one says it.

However, music is considerably different from a visual art such as the motion picture, or drama, and needs further explanation on this matter of the unity of form and content. In and of itself, content in music has been variously described on several levels: the elements of a musical work, the melodies, harmonies, textures, rhythms, and so on; the emotional impact of music; the beauty resulting from formal organization; the story suggested by the music (as in program music); the "vision" of the artist; and the intuitive idea (musical or otherwise) of a work. Everything that is communicated to the listener by the musical work has some validity when we try to describe what in the end is indescribable in words. Content then, exists at various levels and is an attempt to define and understand what the work means. Even in the art of painting, which is not nearly so abstract, one may find many levels of content in a single work. For example, in a highly abstract painting one may show line, space, and color to be the content. But who can say that line, space, and color are no longer the content merely because we recognize the subject in the artist's attempt to show the pathos inherent in the portrait of a face? Line, space, and color are still there and the artist is still concerned with them. They are still content although another level has been added to content—the interpretation of a segment of reality which we recognize as a face. One may see various things in an art work and appreciate it in different ways, depending on what one brings to it in terms of his own experience, talent, and interest. An art work can mean something different to the appreciator than to the artist himself, a trait of all communication, including verbal communication. However, within a given cultural context there will be a general correspondence between the two, even though they are not identical in all details.

Content can be seen not as a specific item but as many items. The content, in being one with its form and expressed through form, may have "meanings" on several levels. One may find musical content to be in a story, on the level of intellectual abstractions of pure melody, in the deep emotion one feels as he listens, or in that vision the composer is trying to express. Music, being the most abstract of all the arts, is particularly suited to embracing various meanings. The form and content are a unity but the form shows a variety of meanings—a variety of contents.

In addition, church music adds the dimension of gospel content to music's variety of meanings. In the incarnation, the church musician finds a perfect expression of content through form, which becomes a model for incarnating his vision through music—a gospel vision inseparable from its musical form. Not that the musical form is able materially to incarnate the gospel, for the form can only embody gospel traits that point to the perfect gospel in the incarnate Christ, but what the musician can do is show the meaning of the gospel implicitly in the medium of music. The form, notes, melodies, rhythms, and harmonies, which are the formal rhetoric of music, inferentially is the gospel content.[9] Music is an analogue of the gospel. It follows, then, that the form must be such that it is capable of embodying the gospel content. This capability is shown as the music participates in the true, honorable, just, pure, lovely, gracious, excellent, and worthy. These are the traits of integrity. They adhere to the universal artistic principles of coherence, unity, continuity, dominance, variety, and tendency gratification established by God in creation.

One would be hard pressed to find an instance when music does not effect a change in the listener. But in the church we often have the notion that effective communication only takes place when one "digs" that which is pretty, familiar, undemanding, popular, and well-liked—a kind of music that sweetens the sourness of the text—a tool that "disarms" the natural resistance of the listener, softening him up for the message. The only criterion for evaluating this music is the degree to which it is liked. The greater the liking the better the communication. Musical communication then boils down to serving up what the people like and want to hear, a kind of musical taste treat that actually turns out to be a continual orgy of musical self-indulgence in which the pastoral ministry of music sinks to acting in the capacity of chef and waiter.

We assume all too readily that music should be patterned after the highly charged verbal barrages to which we are accustomed. But the incarnation as a method of indirect (but relevant) communication which was continued by Jesus himself in His own usage of "cool" non-explicit techniques, such as aphorism, parable, parallel, pun, word play, and story, brings us to the conclusion that indirect methods of communication are most necessary in the church. They are necessary because of the subject matter of our communication and because art and particularly music exist primarily on the implicit, indirect, and inferential level used by our Lord. The criterion for evaluating this music is not the degree to which it pleases, for this places too much emphasis on the music itself, thereby making it highly charged, overpowering, and direct, but the degree to which it has familiarity within the cultural context of its listeners.

To return to this matter of relevancy is important, particularly in light of our discussion of the implicit, less intense level of communication needed in church music, and in the light of the necessity for incarnating gospel content in the music itself. Practically speaking, what do we mean when we say church music should be relevant? Jesus, the incarnate Son, never won any popularity contests, yet He was relevant. Is relevancy just goodness and rightness? If so, God, being ultimate goodness, would not have had to "translate" Himself into human terms. Actually, He was too good, too holy, too much God to be known readily by men, which is the precise reason for the incarnation in the first place.

Relevancy in church music is neither a matter of popularity nor of intrinsic worth, but a matter of identification with the music. That is to say, the music must have something about it which is recognizable and ordinary, both in the configuration of the various musical elements and in its total impact. To begin with, the musical system should normally comply with that found within the general culture. One would not impose a strange musical language—say that of India—on our American church, for our musical system is that of the West. One must also pay attention to the peculiar musical culture of the congregation. This does not necessarily mean their favorite music, or their expectations for a church music, or one's preconceived notions for the music of a certain denomination. It means their actual, real, and exact capability for handling particular musical materials. Obviously a congregation for whom Lawrence Welk or Andrae Crouch is truly high musical art cannot be expected to form an immediate relation to J.S. Bach or Hugo Distler. Knowing the precise skills and aptitudes of a congregation is very important in this matter of relevancy.

We must also deal (like it or not) with the musical mind set of the particular congregation, noting its geographical location, church denomination, social class, average age, taste, general educational level, and its past musical experiences. Taking into consideration these background facts, our biggest and most elusive problem in the area of relevant communication is the closed attitude of many congregations toward that music felt to be appropriate in church. Normally we think of a "certain kind of music" for the Episcopalians, another for the Methodists, another for the Lutherans, another for the Reformed Church, another for the Baptists, and another for the Pentecostals. A psychological barrier is set up so that we predetermine what we will musically respond to in any given situation. Logically this is hardly a total matter of musical aptitude, for there are many people who are well-educated, even musically, who are so conditioned by a certain musical "churchy" mind set that there is only a particular music they will allow themselves to relate to. Often they relate well to great music outside of church, but psychologically shut off their capacity (often unknowingly) in church. The minister of music needs to know this and to use it as part of his total musical understanding of his people. No matter how much he laments such a situation, he will never bring the people around to a more Biblical orientation if he gives up or if he hides his head in the sand. He must face head-on this all too prevalent reality in coming to an informed opinion about musical relevancy for any given congregation.

In coming to know both the congregation's actual musical level and their preferential musical level, a music minister will have a very good beginning for a responsible relevancy. A balance between the two will relieve the musician from basing musical choice on mere taste and give him a wider spread of musical identification possibilities which are necessary to a pastoral ministry of music—a spread in which there will be room for the ordinary, for the implicit, and for the sterling.

It is difficult to know just how far cultural determinism should be accepted as a prime influence on the musical forms that make up our various liturgies. It is true that the situation will determine in large measure the musical form, for music useful in one context is not necessarily useful in another. It may turn out to be completely ludicrous. Even within a single congregation there are differences in age, taste, and cultural conditioning that will affect the choice of music. One needs a certain sense of conglomerate center from which a balanced approach can be taken. In appraising their musical tolerance one observes their level of understanding without losing sight of his musical goals which are determined by his musical and theological vision and standards. God, given His infinite greatness and creativity, could have disclosed Jesus Christ to man in any number of different ways. That He chose the method He did is a picture of the clear understanding God had both of the very nature of man and of Christ's mission. God chose this method because He knew of man's total situation, his creatureliness, his being made in His image, his pride and rebellion, and his mode of living in the world. In freedom, He limited Himself in His revelation to man's situation and fit His communication to man's total condition.

IV. Summary

The incarnation yields a theological groundwork for the church musician in that his attitude must be humble, his stance pastoral. The incarnation is also highly instructive as a method of communication on three main counts. First, God did not hide Himself—He became known on man's level. He became relevant. Musical relevancy is important insofar as the music is within the general cultural context of the congregation. It is not a matter of likes and dislikes but only a matter of familiarity. Music that is completely alien in having no basis for a common understanding (strange to the point of gibberish) denies the incarnation principle. Second, God's coming as a man shows that what music is (its formal worth) defines and embodies meaning (gospel content). To witness to the gospel in terms of music is a matter of truth or integrity. Every piece of music in any given church situation communicates an affirmation or a denial of the gospel. Third, the incarnation in its being an implicit communication gives us necessary insight into the type of communication necessary in church. We should use a music that is ordinary, but not sensational nor laden with overkill. Our concern should be with music that is appropriate to that which it represents, a type of music that invites honest response and active reflection.

In his pastoral capacity, the minister of music leads his congregation with love and is concerned with musical standards only as they reflect what he knows to be spiritual truth within the context of his congregation. The incarnation gives him a basic posture of humility, relevance, and the knowledge that church music must be an understandable "truth" as he goes about his task of ministering.

5

THE GOSPEL
AND CONTEMPORARY CULTURE

I. Music As Witness

Before we evaluate some of the forms of music that are part of contemporary culture's contribution to the church, we should briefly discuss musical witness. As noted in the previous chapter, there must be a certain unity between music (form) and words (content) in which the music and words together complement one another. That is, there must be a unity between what a work says and how it says it. We should not expect a tender love poem set to the march music of John Phillip Sousa to express very much of the sentiment of the text. Nor should the text of "My Last Cigar," "Wouldn't It Be Loverly," or "Houn' Dog" be expressed through a Gregorian chant. In both such cases the music would be so foreign to the idea of the text that gross distortion would result.

The church needs musicians who know what church music should express and who also understand the musical methodology for expressing it. If we think of music as a kind of lubricant and sweetener to get the words "across," we grossly underestimate the nature of music. If we are really concerned with musical witness we must make sure that religious texts have something to say, and then use only music (the medium) that is conformable to that which is being sung. If the gospel is to be witnessed to, the art form itself must effectively reflect it. The words (theology) and music (art) must match.

It cannot be maintained that there must be a specific music for a specific text, but rather that the general category of gospel witness needs music that can effectively personify general theological truth. The medium (music) embodies the gospel content indirectly, the text expresses the gospel directly.

Music articulates in a manner similar to words, in that every musical medium *says* something. Concerning media, Marshall McLuhan has expressed what musicians have long known —"The medium is the message." The medium (music) is not neutral; since it is a dynamic force, it deserves careful consideration. The medium either colors and reinforces the words or it contradicts them. It is the most powerful element in singing. The music swallows the words to the extent that a song is not really the art of poetry or the art of poetry and music: a song is the art of music. Words are important to church music to give *specific* thought content to the gospel and must therefore be highly relevant, but it is the music that actually "carries" the song by its ability to materially represent *general* gospel content. It therefore is mandatory that the church musician understand the basic tenor or feeling tone of the gospel in order for a music to be used which adequately undergirds it, whatever the specific message of the words might be. The characteristics of the gospel must be matched with similar characteristics in the music if the music is to show gospel meaning. In a sense, the music becomes the gospel. It is the gospel in musical action.

II. Gospel Characteristics

Though the attributes of the gospel are many, in the following paragraphs a few will be discussed to give us the general feeling tone or tenor of the gospel. To begin, the gospel of the Lord is universal in scope but personal in application. Christ did not die for the entire human race collectively but individually. Each of us finds in the gospel the unmeasurable riches of God's grace sufficient to meet his own particular personality and need. Furthermore, in Christ we have the capability of fulfilling our potential, of becoming what no one else has been or will be. We are not mere numbers, for Christ knows us by name and gives us the freedom of being ourselves. God lives in and through us, yet we are distinct. He does not require, nor even wish, that we become a standardized product. Each of us is unique and is to bring a further and distinct glory to God's capacity for creating individuality. God's creating is quite different from modern man's mass production techniques. Individual personality remains a very precious part of the creative work of God as shown to us in the gospel of Jesus.

The love of material possessions is a hindrance to full participation in the kingdom. The work of the gospel of the kingdom is the antithesis of making a profit to store up this world's goods. For the Christian, possessions are a means for building up the kingdom. Wealth tends to make claims on its possessor, but the believer, in order to do the will of God, must be free and unshackled from any hindrance. The rich young ruler, as well as Ananias and Sapphira, are Biblical examples of people whose love of money kept them from God's best. The gospel does not tolerate any claim that one of its purposes is the selfish accumulation of this world's goods.

The gospel is the key to full creativity as noted in our discussion of the *Imago Dei*. It encourages the full use of man's gifts as he fulfills his creative responsibility. In being a Christian, one finds that he is truly free from the inside out, free to be uniquely creative and original. The gospel is no cosmetic facelift but a matter of life-changing orientation running deep and swift in its cleansing, shaping, and loving power. It shows to man the fallacy of phoniness and of being concerned for the effect without concern for the cause. The gospel of Jesus Christ stands for integrity, wholeness, and creativity. Genuine newness is the result of an inward dynamic at work—a creativity that breaks new ground with imagination and integrity.

Sacrifice is a basic quality of the gospel. It appears throughout the Bible and culminates in God's ultimate sacrifice of giving His only begotten Son to die a hideous death for our sins. Christ died that we might receive His salvation. Devotion to God on our part likewise requires a self-sacrifice that never wavers. We cannot escape the fact that our interests must serve exclusively God's call. The Lord calls us to serve, not on the basis of what we can get out of it, but on the basis of what we sacrificially have to give.

The gospel costs something in terms of discipleship. Christ's death and resurrection put an awesome responsibility on those who accept Him as Saviour—a responsibility to give Him everything we have and are. Such a calling is often difficult, even painful. To be a disciple is to live a life of self-renunciation, to be a man for others, to leave family, lands, possessions, and friends, to have no other motivation for being except doing the will of the Father. There is a cost to such discipleship and the gospel does not water down the requirements. Few are willing to pay the price. There are no short-cut methods, no easy ways, no getting around the fact that discipleship means discipline.

True discipleship, however, means joy—a deep-seated joy that comes by taking upon oneself Christ's yoke, by doing the will of the Father as revealed in the gospel of Christ. There is a sense of well-being that comes from casting oneself on His love and mercy, from depending on Him for life and sustenance, and from living in the realm of faith where one's whole being is emotionally and intellectually saturated with the presence of God. This joy is not predicated on earthly circumstances or on man himself, but on what Christ has done. It is therefore changeless and undiminished because Christ is ever the same. This joy is not mere amusement, entertainment, or fun; it is beyond description in its depth, and it colors all that one is and does even in his temporal failings and sorrows.

The gospel requires the highest standards of living. Before Christ came murder was prohibited. When He came, however, He taught that to hate another is murder. The Christian is to love his enemies and do good to those who persecute him. He has no personal right to avenge himself. The gospel contains standards that exceed those of the law as well as those of the world. There is no higher calling more stringent than that required of the Christian. And God is the source of this requirement, not man. It is a heavenly calling, a divine standard which consists of what man can accomplish in Jesus Christ—not of what man thinks he is capable of doing by himself.

Integrity is everything to a Christian. His methods and motivations for accomplishing goals are important because the gospel is not so much concerned with achievement as it is with a methodology for living life eternal. A cup of cold water given because one wishes to be seen of men is contrary to everything the Word teaches. One can have the outward display of Christianity, but if he does not manifest the inward work of the Holy Spirit, it is all for nought.

The gospel does not teach that life in Christ should be a continual longing for utopia. Such fantasizing, such avoidance of real living is a romantic escape from the reality of our world, a type of antinomianism that sees our world as something to be shunned. Jesus' teaching, however, is very much concerned with the here and now. We are not to try and escape reality, but to see reality as a gift to be enjoyed and a responsibility to be embraced. To see life as a burden so that fleeing the real world is a prime and attractive activity for the Christian is to wrap oneself into a shell of romanticism which effectively strips the Christian soldier of his concern with living out the full gospel here and now.

Christ asks the best of a man. "Thou shalt love the Lord thy God with all thy heart, soul, mind and strength and thy neighbor as thyself" shows nothing slipshod, second-rate, or inferior about the degree of commitment expected. And it is not a requirement simply asked by God, but demonstrated by Him in the giving of the only begotten Son who gave His all—a complete, full, and perfect work of redemption for man's sin. Such was the case of the widow who gave from her poverty everything she had, a gift which in the Lord's eyes was greater than the rich man's because his gift was but a trifle in comparison with his total wealth. The gospel requires nothing less than our all.

Our Lord taught that the sensational is not the gospel way. The prayer closet is better than righteous display. Whatever we accomplish for the kingdom is not done for the praise of men. Jesus healed and asked that no man be told about it. The gospel is something that is worked out in our lives, not to flaunt, but to serve quietly. The meek way is the gospel way. When good works point to persons, the gospel is violated.

Transience is not a trait of the gospel, for the gospel is changeless. It is given once and for all, and man, taking upon himself the yoke of Christ, takes it once and for all. It is not a matter of easy come, easy go. To decide for Christ is to accept the fact of a life-long relationship in which man becomes conformed to the image of the Son, a process that is not on one day and off the next. The gospel is for the long haul; it is not a modern disposable.

God has made a covenant with man and He discloses His love, mercy, holiness, justice, and power in the gospel of our Lord. Man as a debtor brings nothing to the covenant, but in accepting Christ's redemptive work he takes upon himself the responsibility of living out the gospel in all its fullness. Embracing the Christian faith requires doing, and in the Scripture man finds a composite body of material that tells him how to live in Christ. Man responds to and shows his love for God through a thoughtful commitment to the grace of God, dispensed freely but yet costly. Dietrich Bonhoeffer has written eloquently about formal Christianity which has no commitment. He says that cheap grace is

> the preaching of forgiveness without requiring repentance, baptism without church discipline, Communion without confession, absolution without personal confession. Cheap grace is grace without discipleship, grace without the cross, grace without Jesus Christ, living and incarnate.[1]

He further compares the costly grace of the gospel to

> the treasure trove hidden in the field; for the sake of it a man will gladly go and sell all that he has. It is the pearl of great price to buy which the merchant will sell all his goods. It is the kingly rule of Christ, for whose sake a man will pluck out the eye which causes him to stumble, it is the call of Jesus Christ at which the disciple leaves his nets and follows him.[2]

The gospel is not to be taken lightly. It is given at great price (the life of Jesus Christ) and received in the same spirit (man gives his life to God). The gospel costs everything. It requires the way that fallen man abhors: the hard way, the disciplined way, the sacrificial way, the lonely way, the way of the suffering servant.

These few points might well serve to indicate a basic tenor of the gospel so important for the ministry of music. Here are summaries of a few sample passages which show with particular lucidity such a perspective.

Matthew	4:20-22	The call is to leave possessions and family. Everything is subservient to Christ.
	5:1-12	Blessed are they who practice the God-controlled life as opposed to natural instincts and feelings.
	5:21-26	The stringency of the new standard is shown. Thoughts are as important as deeds.
	5:27-32	Christ gives the command to be pure at great personal cost.
	5:33-37	We are to let our word be binding.
	5:38-42	Give good for evil; go the second mile.
	5:43-48	Love your enemy.
	6:1-4	Live so that men will not praise you.
	6:5-18	The discipline of prayer is to be practiced apart from the praise of men.
	6:19-24	Collection of worldly possessions is not the object in life. It may hinder the real goal.
	7:13-25	Christ's way is lonely as far as great numbers are concerned. Few find the way.
	10:16-39	The world's value system is incompatible to the gospel. Christians will be persecuted.

Such passages suggest that a general tenor or feeling tone of the gospel is an avoidance of popular appeal. Authentic Christianity abhors the enticements of easy acceptance and worldly allurement. The gospel call is one of love *and* one of discipline—a loving discipline that calls us to discipleship in every area of life.

III. Mass Culture

From time to time we have mentioned our general culture in relation to the church. Now we should specifically note that the church, though part of the totality of culture, transcends culture. This knowledge should inspire the body of Christ to share widely and fully its prophetic word, a word divine in its origin, total in its scope, and ultimate in its finality. The church should not be a passive receiver of culture. Rather, it should mold and "salt"culture, impacting it in depth with the full gospel. Problems arise, however, between "earthly" and "heavenly" concerns.

It is these problems between culture and the church we now address. Because some aspects of culture are vividly antireligious, they are easily seen. Consequently believers can strongly oppose them. No Christian needs to be reminded of the church's stance on pornography, drug abuse, political corruption, illiteracy, or crime. Other cultural manifestations, though, have less concern given to them, in spite of the fact that the Bible has much to say about them, and their effect on our society is just as damaging: humanism in education, psychologically oriented do-it-yourself religion, poor stewardship of the earth's resources, materialism, and hedonism. Our particular subject of inquiry (mass culture) is just as obscure because of its harmless (sometimes helpful) appearance, its widespread presence, and its general acceptance. One does not readily perceive its qualities as symptoms of an environmental disease which has made substantial inroads into the church, including the pastoral ministry of music. Our subject is a main motif of our world and has changed the West's way of life greatly. Though not all bad, certain aspects of mass culture have caused the church to renounce much of its own Biblically-based influence for the easier position of swimming uncritically with the cultural current. The church (and church music is not excluded) must reevaluate its position regarding this rapidly moving stream, and if need be, buck the current, rechannel it, or even dry portions of it up. The church must reject the passive role it has often assumed in the name of doing good, and accept its active role which ministers to the whole man and the whole of life. We will attempt to examine this modern day cultural phenomenon, note its characteristics, and assess its position in the musical world as a contributor or hindrance to the gospel of our Lord.

The phenomenon to which we have been referring is "mass culture," *kitsch* if you will. The rise of mass production, mass marketing, and mass media has produced a new society in which the overwhelming spirit is the industrialization of everything, including modern man himself, who is forced into an advocacy of technical and mechanical manipulation and who in turn becomes sub-man, a mere cog in a gigantic operation. Man becomes dehumanized, trivialized, and alienated from his past, his community, his work, and ultimately from himself. He is a slave to a lifestyle that is ordered around a methodology of dealing with a multiplicity of things, everything in life having the mass produced aura. Nothing is exempt. Relationships, work, religion, art, study, and relaxation all gravitate toward a machine orientation that emphasizes speed, quantity, exact timing, technique, and similitude.

The characteristics of mass culture stem from technology and affect our culture in very specific ways, tending to crush the individual, the unusual, and the excellent. Sociologist Ernest van den Haag gives a concise listing of mass culture characteristics:

> Mass culture emphasizes the spectator and the vicarious experience.
> Standardization is a result of trying to please an average of tastes.
> Mass culture shows apathy toward true learning and aims at pleasure, thrill, and escape.
> The market place is the most important factor in mass culture.
> Popular approval is the main moral and aesthetic standard.
> Excessive communication between people tends to weaken the bond between people as the sphere of communication grows larger.
> Mass media replaces the arts.
> Mass culture creates an addiction to prefabricated experience and deprives individuals of autonomous growth and enrichment.[3]

These statements describe the society in which we live, perhaps similar in varying ways to many other cultures in history. Yet the fact is that the influence of the technological business syndrome has made our society different from any other in history.

The arts are not exempt from the influence of mass culture. As a matter of fact, business and industry have latched onto the arts as a lucrative way to turn a profit by becoming commercial controllers of mass culture. The customary answer to the charge of market manipulaton is that they only give the public what it wants, disavowing any culpability in trying to channel taste. However, there are ways of creating demand. First, business knows that the appetites of the public are largely determined by what is already on the market, and second, business promotes vigorously an item which is about to be marketed. H. Radcliff of the Musicians Union maintains that "Any music publisher can tell you six months ahead which tune is going to be popular."[4] This is an overly simplistic generalization, but there is overwhelming evidence that mass man is manipulated far more than he would like to admit.

Commercialization of the arts has lowered artistic standards, encouraged musical tastelessness, and promoted artistic inertia. People involved in commercial enterprise are not aware that there is a vast difference between true art and the commercialized product. Such a distinction is not particularly important in mass culture, because the technician and the mass communicator push the artist into the background with electronic gimmickry, broad exposure, and quick success. Indeed, mass culture is totally success-oriented. Success is the goddess of our society[5] to such an extent that often the only proof of something's validity and value accepted by modern man is soaring sales. One cannot argue with success at the cash register.

Strangely enough, one of the biggest problems we have in our society is not a dearth of music, but too much. Music of all kinds is used for environmental backround. Music then becomes muzak and is not to be listened to (that is, listened to with the critical faculties of one's whole person), but rather to be used as environment, just to be there, unobtrusively in the background like pastel colors on a wall. The only time when one notices it is when it stops and silence results. Many Americans rise to muzak, eat to muzak, drive to muzak, work to muzak, entertain to muzak, and go to sleep to muzak. It is simply everywhere. In a scathing attack on this "sewage system of sound," Paul Hindemith shows how damaging it can be to one's listening habits and compares it to brainwashing.[6] It affects our musical sensibilities to the point that great music has little chance to speak to us because muzak dulls and conditions our minds and emotions into a senseless state through the continual noisy barrage of sensual sound. We not only cease to listen, we cease to hear. We become musically comatose.

> Most of us, surrounded as we are by music almost as inescapably as by air, have successfully pushed it into the background of our consciousness. This is often a matter of simple self-defense. Inferior music beats at our ears in a dreary whine in the home, in stores, and on the streets. Who would wish to listen attentively to this, much less think deeply about it?[7]

Our technology has served to aggravate this problem with the invention of recording and playback equipment, the availability of canned music, and the business enterprises that are formed to make a profit selling, dispensing, and repairing the electronic systems, as well as choosing and programming the musical compositions which are to do "the job." Businesses use muzak because they think people work more efficiently by listening to music. At least, experiments seem to indicate an improved productivity. Business people therefore reaffirm the idea that the increasing of industrial yield is all important, even to the point of meriting the prostitution of the arts. Some churches even go along with mass culture's love affair with muzak by installing speakers in every nook and cranny of their building complex, by acquiring a suitable record library, and by operating the system almost continually from morning until night or as long as a single person is within hearing range. Even the worship service is not exempt. People who are conditioned to this continual sound become less and less capable of understanding and appreciating the true and full meaning of music and develop the psychological problem of being afraid of silence.

IV. The Church and Mass Culture

The main motif of our society, mass culture, confronts the church with many problems. How can the church be in the world yet not be conformed to the world? How can it actively witness to the world but not become identical with it? John Robinson feels that the church might play a role analogous to that of the Communist party in Soviet Russia, where the small minority wields influence out of proportion to its size.[8] The church, though small in number, could be a powerful force to aid in the formulation of a healthier culture. But this does not answer the question as to what the church's all-inclusive attitude should be toward the general culture. It cannot cut itself off from culture or it will have no ministering place. But it likewise cannot be one with it, for then the church will have nothing prophetic to say. We are to be in the world, but not of the world; the church is caught in the middle. And that seems to be the best answer: to understand the betwixtness and betweenness in a positive way, as a creative counterpoint. There are

> churches which have endeavored to enter into the life of the world and bear witness to the relevance of Christian faith for the totality of human existence without themselves becoming captive to the values and idolatry of the world. Such churches have understood the normative relationship between the church and the world in terms of creative *tension* or polarity.[9]

It is this tension between the world and the divine mission of the church that can bring it to a place of fulfilling the great commission without asetheticism or worldliness. The church cannot accept unjudiciously cultural forms that are alien to the message it is trying to proclaim. Mass culture has some good aspects the church can profitably use, but the degrading emphasis of *kitsch* that affects so much of the church's life must be recognized, understood, and evaluated from a Biblical perspective and then action taken depending on the results of one's analysis. The church must witness to culture through culture—but not uncritically. The distinctives of the gospel must be maintained.

V. Pop Music Characteristics

Mass culture, having had its beginnings in the industrial revolution, has taken a long time to come to its present state. Since its inception, however, it has gradually and increasingly influenced the art forms of our culture. Mass culture has fostered a new genre—pop music. Pop music has in fact become a musical mirror of the heart of this society, the musical embodiment of *kitsch*.

Of course popular music was in existence long before the advent of mass culture. Indeed, some musicians are fond of citing Luther's use of *contrafacta* (putting religious words to a pre-existent "secular" tune) as a justification for their use of modern day pop. But the thrust of the popular music of Luther's time and the thrust of our pop music is as different as night is from day. There was a stylistic unity in the sixteenth-century musical world between the various genres of music which no longer exists in today's music: "there was little difference between the features of a melody originally associated with a secular text and one written particularly for a sacred text."[10] Church songs based on Gregorian chant exhibited the same musical traits as those coming from the popular music of the day. "A difference in style between sacred and secular music hardly existed."[11] The popular music of the time had a folk-like character far removed from modern day pop. It was not until the advent of technology that the music which we refer to as pop began —a combined expression of the machine and technocratic man.

The word *popular* needs to be defined. It is a neutral term which simply means "something that is in demand." However, in order to understand what we mean by the word *pop*, the word *popular* will be used as a technical term, indicating that which is distinctly manufactured for widespread acceptance. It is intended to mean that which is created to be popular rather than that which incidentally has become popular.[12] This usage of the word *popular* refers more to the characteristics of the art form than to what has become of the art form.

So that we might come to grips with this musical art form of mass culture as one possibility for setting gospel texts (remember, we seek a unity between the words and the music), we must analyze the characteristics of pop music in more detail, for what we wish to discover is how closely pop music characteristics are to the gospel characteristics already enumerated. We then will be better able to judge pop music's ability to musically express a gospel text. No doubt we will have to make some generalizations, but keeping in mind our definition of pop, we can speak with a fair degree of accuracy. The traits we will investigate are numerous and often difficult to pinpoint. However, there are certain overall traits that occur often enough to be highly visible.

The most obvious trait of pop music is that it is an item of quantity. The object is produced with shortcut techniques, resulting in great profusion. It is manufactured wholesale. The mass production system of pop music is clearly shown by Paul Hindemith:

> One shows how denaturized an art can become once it is made a part of an industrial production system totally inhuman and dictatorial. In Hollywood, they keep composers and arrangers in little booths provided with staff paper and piano, and here on the assembly-line music is produced in which all the normal virtues that are part and parcel of the composer's profession—imagination, enthusiasm, original talent—are just so many factors hindering industrial production.[13]

The commercial assembly line is a feature of pop creation in which each part of the work, such as melody, harmony, orchestration, and so on, may be the responsibility of its own "specialist." Rather than carrying through with his own creation, the composer farms it out to those who can do it more quickly and easily because there is no need for holistic integrity or originality.

Popular music in America is big business, run by the methods and techniques of big business for the sake of huge financial rewards. A distinct science of marketing and popularization procedure is part of the commercial influence. The tradition of Tin Pan Alley continues where composers "[grind] out their songs with mechanical precision and with the principal goal of achieving a huge sheet-music and record sale."[14] Pop music is molded into "patterns of 'commercial' banality."[15]

The popular has an incredible drive toward continuous novelty. Durability and depth are not characteristics of its products. Wearing out soon, they must be quickly replaced. In order for pop to continue to grab the attention of the public on whom it feeds, it must ever produce a new twist, a glossed over cliché, or even outright shock. In its novelty, it shows itself to be shallow musically, for novelty is merely repetition in a different but quickly recognizable disguise—a surface change without substance. Being novel is the closest it can become to being creative.

Pop music does not wear well because the actual musical content (melody, harmony, rhythm, form) is fairly standardized. There is "nothing inherently different between one 'pop' tune and another."[16] Since pop music contains nothing intrinsically new or creative, maximum musical gratification comes immediately. Pop music thus promotes further musical immaturity. Our culture, which is concerned with the now and with the self, readily identifies with this pop syndrome because to delay gratification of any kind is anathema. "Give me what I want now, without cost, without travail, without effort." The need for immediate gratification based on well worn, tried and true musical conventionalities must be appeased. As a matter of fact, some feel that "the fundamental characteristic of popular music [is] standardization."[17]

Ease of consumption is another aspect of the popular. The object asks little of the consumer. It is made so that easy assimilation can take place. Thus efforts are spared and shortcuts are chosen in order that satisfaction may be achieved in a direct, convenient, and non-taxing manner. The presupposition of *kitsch* is that predigestion be a distinctive feature of aesthetic quality. There is little in the way of a challenge to the listener. If music is to operate on the popular level, music education becomes totally unnecessary.[18] There is nothing of musical significance to learn. One can forget the discipline of musical art because that which is made for consumption requires little in the way of mind or emotion.

Entertainment is one of the obvious characteristics of pop music. In aiming at pleasure and satisfaction on the immediate level, it dispenses with good taste. Pop music seeks fun and amusement at the expense of beauty. Titilation through emotionalism, bypassing the intellect, is this music's *raison d'etre*. Because it is so pervasive, entertainment enters into the thought, feeling, and world view of the listener, who, as a consumer, defines his very existence by these "pleasurable" experiences. Modern popular culture "seeks not to encourage reflection, criticism, or discrimination, but to reduce as many serious issues as possible to the level of entertainment."[19] The more society becomes *kitsch*, the greater the danger of its aiming at the lowest common denominator. The popular does not merely try for the *average*, but actively promotes the lesser. The lowest standard becomes the norm. It does this because the path of least resistance requires little in the way of musical artistry from the listener. In requiring little from him, this music entertains man and encourages musical slothfulness. His stewardship of the heart and mind given to him by God is degraded. Creativity, integrity, and honesty are but theoretical concepts which hinder artistic apathy. Pop preys upon man's fallen condition, tending to exploit his weakness for the easy way.

The popular is success-oriented. Success is measured in terms of numbers and money, and without success the popular has no support and dies a quick death. Thus a basic aim of the popular must be to do only that which will appeal—generally what is musically safe and unprovocative. The overriding concern is profit, and when that begins to wither away, the art form also withers and dies. It stands not on its own artistic merits but on its ability to sell. There is nothing so stone cold and worthless as yesterday's pop hit.

There are elements of romanticism in the popular. Pop music tends to retard emotional maturity and invites unrealized idealization. The characteristics of romanticism in literature, delineated by C.S. Lewis, are themes similarly found in the popular: the dangerous or adventurous, the marvelous, the subjective, the rebellious in respect to civilization or convention, the sensitivity to natural objects, the association with solemnity and enthusiasm, intense longing which is prized for itself, and mystery in the thing longed for.[20] In music, the pop field is more concerned with fantasy than with reality. Often its theme is that which cannot be.

The popular creates an environment inhospitable to quality. Often great artists refuse to acquiesce to the popularisms of their day, because faithfulness to integrity often demands the sacrifice of popular appeal. The true artist's purpose is not to find a comfortable berth in the world or to achieve popular recognition, but to get his creative work done.[21] Mediocrity, however, is the standard of the popular. The commercial music industry tries its very best to offend very few, resulting in a middle-of-the-road approach in which an indifference to values, standards, and principles sets in. One cannot create something for popularity without a calculated effort to dispose of universal artistic norms. The only thing that flourishes without critical evaluation is mediocrity.

The popular capitalizes on sensationalism. Musical presentation is seen as a packaged product complete with light displays, dazzling costumes, electronic modification and augmentation, decibel overkill, and stage gimmicks. The popular is not only vulgar, but it encourages fantasies of grandeur, appeals to the sensuous, exaggerates, and is associated with extravagance and infantilism. Hyped-up performance is much more important than the inherent quality of the art form. In pop music, slicked-up arrangements of aesthetic monstrosities are standard fare.

The popular is the epitome of transience. Pop music cannot be anything else, for to be popular is to affirm expendability. The "Top 40 Hits" change from week to week, wearing thin very quickly. Having no depth, the popular must depend on its disposability to continue the genre.

Many of these qualities of popular music stem from the drive to make this art form primarily a means of monetary gain, which is to say that its overall quality is to be found in the area of commercialization. In very direct language, Arthur Korb states that popular music is "written and published primarily to make money."[22] A pop composer treats his music not as an art but as a commodity:

> A [popular] song writer must learn to become a business man—a clever businessman who will handle himself successfully and make the cash registers keep on ringing up the sales. Your songs are a commodity that you will be placing on the selling market.[23]

The composer barters his artistic integrity in exchange for general acceptance from the masses.

The phrase, "general and immediate appeal to the widest audience" is in fact not only a description of the pop song; it is also a definition of the word *commercial*, and it's a phrase you better get your teeth into right now. Publisher experience over the years shows that the pop type of tune has the widest appeal, as proved by hard cash over the counter. All pop tunes are therefore commercial. They are the most saleable in the market, the most "popular" (which gives you the origin of the word pop).[24]

To write pop music successfully, one must strive to write music that pleases the widest audience. The composer is no longer his own man, for every creative impulse must be checked by "What will they think?" "Will they like it?" and "Will it sell?" After a while, composers give up trying for creative integrity (if they ever tried it in the first place) and fall into the much easier method of writing by use of tried and true stock formulas. Many song writers (often those with the most number of "successes") are technically incompetent. Some cannot read music, let alone write it. They fall into the pattern popularized (but not begun by) the pop composers of the 1890's who began to "compose" by melodic, harmonic, and rhythmic standardization to the extent that not even a scant knowledge of music theory was necessary to mass produce what the public was to buy and then inevitably to discard. "The very climate of the pop music business discourages the nurturing of skill and inspiration. There is a built-in expendability both of materials and artist—neither is expected to last the pace for long."[25] The sacrifice of artistic integrity to create pop music is a high price for the artist to pay. It is tantamount (by way of comparision) to selling his soul. No artist can afford the loss of his creative insight.

It is important to mention that simplicity is not necessarily a basic characteristic of the popular. In our complex technological society, that which is simple is often automatically placed in a "light" or "popular" category. It is true that much pop music exhibits simplicity. However, great music can also be simple. Complex and simple are not analogous to artistic and popular or to good and bad.

Like *popular*, the word *contemporary* is often used to describe modern-day religious pop. This is a misnomer, however. *Contemporary* is best used as a technical term describing any musical form whose compositional elements (harmony, rhythm, melody, counterpoint) are characteristic of twentieth-century theoretical practice. It is confusing to consider both Daniel Pinkham and William Gaither, for example, as composers of "contemporary" music. True, both are currently writing, but their individual classifications of compositional technique are quite different—the former is based in the twentieth-century (hence contemporary) and the latter, like most composers of religious pop, is based in the common-practice period procedures of the seventeenth, eighteenth, and nineteenth centuries, with some modifications of course. The term "now generation" to describe this genre would be more accurate and would lessen the confusion surrounding the word "contemporary."

Much more could be said about the whole technological-business syndrome, but for our purposes enough has been said to get at the question of the validity of pop for use in a pastoral ministry of music. We have noted that pop music is concerned with quantity (mass production), material profit, novelty, immediate gratification, ease of consumption, entertainment, the lowest common denominator, success first of all, romanticism, mediocrity, sensationalism, and transience. Its basic impetus and overall quality is to be found in the drive for making money. It is a commercial music. One can see in these characteristics a clear relationship to the characteristics of mass culture in general. Pop music is indeed the musical articulation of the latter. On the other hand, the gospel is concerned with individuality, non-materialism, creativity, sacrifice, discipleship, joy, high standards, principles above success, reality, encouragement of the best, meekness and permanence. Its overall thrust is a free salvation which opens to man a joyous life of loving selflessness and discipline in which man does the will of the Father. The gospel was not made for popular approval or widespread acceptance without cost, for "narrow is the way and few there be who find it." If these characteristics were placed side by side they would look like this:

Gospel Characteristics	Pop Music Characteristics
Individuality	Quantity
Non-materialism	Material profit
Creativity	Novelty
Sacrifice	Immediate gratification
Discipleship	Ease of consumption
Joy	Entertainment
High standards	Least common denominator
Principles above success	Success first of all
Reality	Romanticism
Encouragement of the best	Mediocrity
Meekness	Sensationalism
Permanence	Transience

It is readily apparent that the gospel characteristics are diametrically opposed to those of pop music, leading one to the conclusion that if music is to be analogically related to the message of the words, then there is no possibility whatsoever of successfully matching the two in a pop song. Pop music does away with everything in the way of musical goodness for the sake of being popular. The gospel stands for everything alien to popularity. To try to force a gospel text into a pop music mold is to force it into something that it is ill-suited to occupy. It seems absolutely imperative to conclude that to use pop music as a medium for the gospel message is wrong. It is wrong because the music has inherently those characteristics that are contrary to what the words mean. The medium, in terms of pop music, kills the message.

VI. The Church and Pop

The church musician involved in the pastoral ministry of music may feel quite apart from all of this. After all, he does not use the "Top 40" in church. Therefore, what is the point of it all? The point is this: the pop music syndrome has been part of the church music field for over a century beginning with the stock formula gospel song, and it has gradually become the most important single artistic influence on many, if not most, churches. That is to say, the majority of music in evangelical churches has been patterned after the music of the pop world. Of course, if the whole point of the church and the gospel were popularity, then there would be no other way to go musically. However, this is not the mission of the church.

Church pop is that music which has exactly the same musical qualities as "secular" pop. There is a general aura of superficiality in which rhythmic, harmonic, and melodic elements are blended into a kind of musical banality which is the stuff of pop music's characteristics. Quite often such pop music enters the church long after its introduction into the general music scene, for in the church's lack of genuine creativity it has not even the fortitude to copy the world until the new pop becomes "old hat." Such was the case with rock music, for example. For a time it was considered off-limits, even sinful.[26] Converted rock musicians often went around preaching against it and then demonstrated in their own music a lack of musical creativity. In fact, in many cases their music was far inferior to that which they were preaching against. Eventually, however, rock music was not only accepted but used as one of the many popular stylistic bases which church composers took over, diluted, sweetened, and sentimentalized. It was often called the church's own, but it would have been better to have left it where it was and what it was.

Pop music (often termed "contemporary sound" but for our use anything which is created to be popular thus affecting its musical characterisitics) is so widespread that many musicians and churches use nothing else. There are children growing up who will never know the Christian faith (in terms of music) as anything but musical tawdriness. The convoluted irony of this is that they do not realize it because they have never heard anything else, while creators of such musical inferiority are usually well aware of what great church music is. One of the composers of "folk" musicals, in remarks before a denominational church music conference, noted that

> What we are doing is not necessarily great music. It is music that does work. And it is music that does seem to bring about results. But we . . . realize that there is great, great music which you should be performing with your young people.[27]

The great tragedy is that though the worth of great music is often realized by composers of church pop, the pragmatic rationale of "doing what works" when composing pop becomes the rationale of the local church music director in performing it. This leads directly into a continuation and augmentation of such a rationale, because pop has a way of propagating its own by swallowing and exterminating better musical expression. (The token performance of an *a cappella* motet or a Bach chorale is not the answer, for it is looked upon as a bitter medicine taken only to appease the musical "highbrow." Great music does not become a natural musical expression.) The way of least resistance is to omit anything of musical significance, which shortchanges the entire congregation, from children to adults.

One can hardly blame the local music director and congregation for such a pathetic situation, though they share part of the responsibility. The powerful business influences at work on man's predilection for ease create such irresistible forces that the Christian church is swept off its feet. That which is offered is readily apprehensible, light, attractively packaged, and entertaining. Stars jet around the country singing and playing gospel concerts (for a very good monetary return) complete with advance men, local organization, advertising media, record albums and tapes, and autographed pictures. They put on a publicity campaign to rival that of a political candidate. Press releases, conferences, and interviews give the "star" wide exposure and stardust class. Sheet music, anthem arrangements, tape accompaniments, and publisher-sponsored reading sessions with powerfully merchandised advertising techniques, increase this music's influence on the entire church. Ultimately the church is hooked. Could popular acclaim be wrong? Well, one can hardly argue with success. As they say, "He might be wrong, but he laughs all the way to the bank!" The accolades and adulation of the crowd, the respect of the public, the gratitude of the clergy, the crowded schedules, the growing independence of the booking agent, all serve to validate the star and his music. Is it any wonder the church wilts under such prestigious influence?

Unfortunately this scenario is played out variously on both larger and smaller scales. The "give them what they want" of pop music finds its way into every musical endeavor. Religious publishing firms, often castigated for being mainly interested in profits, obviously do not bear total responsibility for church music's dependence on pop, but they should take seriously some small obligation to help the church in a more responsible way. If they only supply what sells the best without attempting to publish better music for a more mature ministry of music (even if it is not on the best seller list), then the accusation is justified. An inbred syndrome of supply-creates-demand sets in and mature musical ministry is inhibited.

Many individual church pop musicians might also see their work more honestly as simple entertainment rather than trying to persuade others of their "ministering." People who glamorize and idolize such entertainers should know and accept them for what they are and then should open their minds and hearts to other possibilities for music in the church.

The director of music might become less dependent on the works of pop musicians and systematically begin to bring depth into the music of his congregation and choir, knowing full well that his own popular "rating" will go down. But if there is anything to this matter of actual musical ministry, because of his dealing in musical symbols more than verbal ones, he must come to grips with the musical language first, because that is his specific and special way of being the truth, of witnessing to the gospel of Christ. The medium of music is witness and it should not be desecrated by attempting to be like the pop music and pop culture of our day.

VII. Methodological Questions

What about the thousands of blessings, conversions, and deeper commitments effected by the world of pop? After all, if it works does not that prove its validity? Surely the church needs every advantage it can get in this world of darkness. The argument that man can make nothing which is intrinsically worthy of God is often used. Therefore, why struggle and strain against the swiftly running stream of pop? Since we cannot do anything intrinsically worthy of God, since pop is a favorite, light and entertaining music, and since it works, why should we question its use?

These questions are among the first to be heard whenever there is a difference of opinion on church music matters. In our pragmatic, success-oriented society, the general feeling is that whatever brings one to faith, or affects a person positively toward a God-centered orientation, is not only all right but should be actively promoted. However, if results always dictated our methodology, all culture, including religion, would depend more on man's fallen state than upon Biblical principles, a situation which is happening more and more in our world.

Good results can be attained with incorrect methods. For example, Moses was instructed by God to speak to the rock for water to quench the thirst of the children of Israel; instead he disobeyed and smote the rock with his rod. Water still came—he got the desired result. Another example is Judas, who carried out a most despicable act of betrayal leading to the crucifixion of our Lord which made possible salvation, but who was held responsible by God for his act even though it was used as a methodological tool in God's plan of salvation.

God is sovereign. He can use anything to bring glory to His name and to accomplish His will: the disobedience of Moses, the suffering of Job, the infidelity of Judas. He can use whatever man gives Him—even if it is only the merest pittance. But this does not excuse man from being and doing what God wants. St. Paul did not encourage the Roman Christians to continue in sin that grace might abound that much more. "God forbid," he said. Man is still responsible for his actions and he will have to answer for them, results or not! Because of his disobedience, Moses was prohibited from entering the promised land. Judas went out and hanged himself. The fact that God's sovereignty is not dependent on man's right action is no reason to think that God is uninterested in methodology. He is simply not bound by it. If He were, He would not be God. Therefore, the fact that something "works" is more a statement about God's sovereignty and His use of what man in human poverty provides Him than a validation of the particular method or practice in question.

Good methodology is Christian action freely cognizant of all the implications of one's doing. Right methods are absolutely vital because they are indications of our obedience to our understanding of Biblical revelation. The Bible itself, a book of God's just dealings with man in history, was given to teach us how to live. Its principles are to carry through in all of life—even in our music. Our methodology must have the qualities of that which we hope to accomplish (that is, honest and good communication for the gospel's sake as opposed to musical hucksterism or musical enticement). But more than that, it must be an indication of a right and obedient stand before God. The gospel principles enumerated earlier should not, in terms of music, be conformed to this world, but should be transformed into the musical essence of those gospel principles. Methods are in man's hands—results are in God's.

The church musician is going to have to answer to God for his methods even as Moses did. He will not escape judgment. To think that anything is all right simply because it works is to completely misunderstand gospel witness. Pop music is alien to the gospel (remember its musical characteristics to which we referred) and is useless in the pastoral ministry of music.

VIII. Folk Music and Jazz

There are two other types of musical expression which should be briefly examined, for they often come up in the same context as pop music—folk music and jazz. Folk music has always been a distinct part of man's culture. It has influenced art music of all ages, sometimes as a moderating influence, sometimes as raw material for musical composition, and sometimes as the genesis of virile and independent musical systems or part of systems.

Folk music must be sharply distinguished from popular music of the type under consideration in two important respects. First, folk music is primarily that which arises from a particular culture, often without known composers. It is music that is primarily transmitted through aural tradition and is shaped and reshaped as it is passed on from generation to generation. It may have a variety of purposes, but it is primarily music that is utilitarian; that is, the aesthetic quality is blended into the unity of man's daily life. It is not music to eat by or to listen to in a concert hall. It is music to participate in. Thus, there arises a body of music that has wide acceptance, grows and changes slowly, and broadly shows the primitive thought of its culture about such things as birth, death, love, work and play, success and failure, hope and despair.

The second distinguishing mark between folk music and pop music is the absence of commercialism in the former. Folk music has no "professional composers" and is not a music for the purpose of making a profit. It is not a commodity one tries to sell. Therefore, its popularity does not rest on its being made in a certain way so that it will be popular. There is no thought of "doing things" to the art form for predetermined ends. Folk music is popular in the sense that it is of the people and not foisted on the people. It is part of the evolutionary process of culture. The integrity of the music lies in its faithful mirroring of common musical usages.

Often folk tunes are used as raw material for more popular musical expressions. Roy Harris notes:

> When Broadway seemed to be running out of material, some of the smart songwriters decided to make a raid on the virgin soil of American primitive folk song. Today the air waves are flooded with commercial versions of old folk tunes set to June-moon-swoon rhymes, sung by confection-mike voices accompanied by slick bands.[28]

Such procedures as ironing out the rhythms into some type of even arrangement, changing or adding harmony, or rewriting the tune are often used. By the time the folk song has been rehashed, the face-lifting is so complete that often the original freshness, spontaneity, and earthy quality have been completely incinerated.

Folk songs are usually strophic, sometimes modal, rhythmically free, and predominantly monophonic. Many of them resemble plainsong, the music of the church historically being heavily influenced by folk music.[29] Their greatness is in their utter simplicity. Artlessness is their strength. This type of music is never pretentious, sensational, or maudlin; it is earthy and wholesome.

Folk music seems to be an ideal form of religious music. It shows unique traits of creativity that are fresh and vital. The music, being music of integrity, is able to carry the Christian message well. Its simplicity and directness add to its strength. In a sense, the gospel is utterly simple so that a child can receive it, and folk music emphasizes this aspect of the gospel better than any other music. It also shows, in terms of music, the wide invitation for all to come to Christ, for folk music, because it is a music of the people and not a sophisticated music, does not have class bias; it appeals to the cultured music lover as well as to the uncultured.

There is always the tendency, however, for people to "sophisticate" this music, to "make it better." Such well-meaning attempts often end up vulgarizing a perfectly valid medium. Routley shows that Geoffrey Beaumont's *Folk Mass,* the granddaddy of the current fad for religious "commercial folk," is not folk music at all except for a few passages.[30] In our time, folk music has been subjected to all types of manipulation. Such forms as "folk-musicals," "folk-rock," and "gospel-folk" are slicked-up renditions of the folk style. Such adaptations are more commercial and pop than "folk," and often use the name "folk" solely for the purpose of sales appeal. They have very few of the musical characteristics of folk but around in pop manifestations.

Another kind of musical genre that often comes up in the context of popular music is jazz. André Hodeir, in chronicling its history, says that jazz has gone through an artistic evolution.[31] New forms, building on old forms (much the same as development in general musical history), were continuously being improved, so that jazz, which began as musically uninteresting material, gradually became music of artistic merit and genius. Leonard Bernstein says:

The jazz player has become a highly serious person. He may even be an intellectual. He tends to wear Ivy-League clothes, have a crew cut, or even wear horn-rimmed glasses. He may have studied music at a conservatory or a university. This was unthinkable in the old days. Our new jazzman plays more quietly, with greater concentration on musical values, on tone quality, technique. He knows Bartok and Stravinsky, and his music shows it.[32]

Jazz is an indigenous American music and must be considered to have achieved the state of a serious art form. Indeed the harmonic and contrapuntal foundations of "progressive" jazz are extremely intricate and the performance requirements so high that only the technically competent are able to play well this type of music. Jazz, therefore, is musically definable and has become a great musical expression in its own right.

Jazz, like folk music, must be distinguished from our definition of pop music. As modern jazz developed into serious musical expression, it found difficulty in achieving

popularity without forsaking the achievements of modern jazz. Since the end of the war only a very few jazz musicians—and not always the best—have managed to find favor with the general public who, in any case, prefers the howling idols of rock 'n roll.[33]

Jazz has achieved the status of art music at the expense of popularity. To try for mass appeal, contemporary jazz would have to sacrifice the values and principles which have made it great. We must conclude that popular music and jazz are far from being the same thing, for jazz is a much richer music than pop, both aesthetically and emotionally.

Like all music, jazz is uneven in its quality. Some of it is very bad, showing traits like those of pop. But it is a young expression and as it develops along the lines of integrity, more and more of it will be adaptable to situations calling for greatness. Good jazz is compatible with the gospel because it is good art, having musical worth, and has a place in the church's musical expressions.

In their encounter with jazz, Christians may embrace it as part of their culture, part of the goodness of God's created world. But unlike pop music, it is not merely a commodity designed for consumption; its purpose goes deeper than escape or entertainment.[34]

There is also the matter of association. For many people, the word *jazz* conjures up a picture of smoke-filled dance floors, dimly lit bars and scantily dressed waitresses. If such negative connections are made by a congregation then obviously it will not be for them the powerful expression of gospel witness it otherwise might have been. In such cases it is better to find a more acceptable alternative than to force the issue. It is ironic, though, that many who reject jazz outright embrace the more widely accepted music of rock 'n roll (with Christian words, of course), a pop form which has such a sordid social and musical history that its use in the church would be scandalous to the average congregation should the truth about it be known.

IX. Summary:
An Urgent Theological Resolve

The spirit of our time is primarily that of industrial society which dehumanizes man with mass-production systems and entices him into a machine-like orientation. Technology has come to play an increasingly large role in the musical world, not only in the mechanical production of records, tapes, listening systems, radio, and television, but also in the composition of music. We see mass culture's influence in pop music as it combines contrived musical clichés, production line method, and business commercialization. Society in general and the church in particular have become unknowing connoisseurs of musical mediocrity. A century ago many branches of the evangelical church adopted a musical posture of embracing the pop style gospel song. Thousands of these religious pop songs were mass produced, published, and marketed so that entire generations were brought up solely on the tunes of "In the Garden," "The Old Rugged Cross," "At the Threshold,"[35] and "Shall We Gather At the River?" What they were brought up with became the standard to be perpetuated. It was only during the latter part of the 1950s and 1960s that new musical expressions were reluctantly admitted into many evangelical churches and only after much travail. Even then new pop styles made most of the inroads. Now this newer pop genre is being perpetuated. Those currently in the pastoral ministry of music must make a conscious effort to affirm other, more worthy and true musical expressions and to return pop to its rightful place within our culture.

Music, like the gospel, can never come cheaply or easily, either in its creation or in its appreciation. Church music must affirm creativity and discourage commercial banality as it impacts culture. Let the church scatter the salt of the gospel with artistic wholeness and integrity. The message is *in* the medium.

6

FAITH

I. The Wholeness of the Christian Life

The theme of faith is familiar to all church goers. Many church school lessons and sermons have exhorted the believer to "have faith," if he would "move mountains." Our treatment of the term will be broader than this general usage. Here, the word *faith* will be used in two interdependent ways: (1) as a general mode of Christian being, and (2) as a specific type of action. The first, faith as a general mode of being, refers to the Christian faith, the life of faith, or the life in faith. The second, faith action, involves stepping into the unknown, walking "blindly," or living by absolute trust in one's certain knowledge of God.

The life of faith as we are using the term is a fundamental attitude or outlook on life in which one's world view has been reoriented and centered around the Creator. A person's stance toward the world and his living in it is holistic—he neither curses the world nor resigns himself to it, but sees all of life as a gift to be developed profitably for glorifying the Creator. The Christian faith puts together the fragmented pieces of life as the Christian comes to know purpose, meaning, and order. With a perspective derived from Christ, all of life is a manifestation of the eternal and will corroborate the central thesis that God is the Creator who loves us, has redeemed us, has promised healing for man's broken self, and has given the world as a gift and a responsibility.

The Christian's life, then, is a wholly integrated existence. There ought to be no barriers, no imbalances, no compartments. His total life is lived in Christ and everything the Christian does is centered around this perspective. As Herbert W. Farmer has said, the Christian life is "the massive unity."[1]

Two problems in church music illustrate the widespread assault on the wholeness of the Christian life. The first problem centers on sacred-secular life compartmentalization. The second problem deals with the imbalance of emotion and reason (in music and religion) in holistic living.

First, the unity of life lived in faith is often fragmented by a sacred-secular dichotomy in which we give some parts of our existence a sacred or religious label and others a secular or worldly label. However, these boundaries are artificial at best. For the Christian, nothing is exempt from the unity of the life in faith. If anything is part of him, it is part of his faith life. All that he is and does is sacred because of his orientation around the Source and Center of his life, Jesus Christ.

Music in the church has always been embroiled in this sacred-secular debate. The early church fathers attempted to be clear in their distinction between sacred and secular music. Through the centuries, the church has tried to protect "its" music from the influence of the "world," but has only succeeded in being behind the times. Most musical developments have taken place outside the mainstream of church life and have been assimilated only gradually and with great reluctance (howbeit steadily and systematically) at the insistence of composers. In our time the debate rages on, though in the sixties and seventies we have had more freedom (as far as the sacred-secular controversy is concerned) than ever before. Still, there are those who see certain genres of music as secular, and for that reason they ban them from worship, while other classes of composition (irrespective of any other consideration) are welcomed in a wholesale manner because of their "sacredness."

Actually, one is at a loss to explain what it is that is supposed to make music in and of itself sacred or secular. The usual explanations, such as words, style, compositional devices, sincerity, artistic value (or lack of it), and religious orientation of the composer, ultimately are all unsatisfactory. We agree with Paul Henry Lang who has shown that it is impossible to establish a set of rules for making music "sacred," and who, therefore, suggests the term be avoided.[2] After all, the stuff of music (time and tone) are not religious or profane but amoral. If the raw material of music cannot be considered sacred or secular then the finished product in and of itself is "neither sacred or secular; it is only interesting or dull, polyphonic or monophonic, accompanied or *a cappella,* and so on."[3]

"Sacred" and "secular" are not qualities of things; they are qualities of relationship orientation. For example, one cannot paint a Christian landscape but one can view it in a Christian way, for what the beholder brings to the encounter determines its sacred or secular quality. Thus the terms *sacred* and *secular* are better used in conjunction with a mode of existence—namely one's basic orientation as either sacred or secular. For the Christian, then, life in its entirety is sacred. He has no compartments; his work, his recreation, his relationships, his art, and his music are seen through life in Christ.

This is not to suggest that church music standards should be abolished—far from it! But a recognition that what one brings to the music determines its "sacredness" rather than "sacredness" being a property of the music itself, not only opens up for many congregations a vast store of music hitherto untouched because of sacred-secular restrictions, but also gives a unification, an orientation, and a Christian purpose to all of one's music making. Musical choice will not be made on the basis of sacred-secular categories but on music's ability to stand the scrutiny of one's musical-theological judgments. That which is worthy will be hallowed by virtue of the consecration of the musician and that which is unworthy will be discarded. The result will be a complete and total music-life unity in which the life in faith from beginning to end, from top to bottom, in and out, through and through, will be seen as wholly consecrated—in a word, *sacred.*

In respect to the second problem relating to the imbalances which threaten holistic living, it must be said that man consists of mind and emotion in inseparable unity. Dividing him into isolated segments as we are so prone to do gives a distorted picture of the wholeness that is his God-given characteristic. Man knows and feels; he feels and knows. Mind acts upon emotion, and emotion upon mind. Each contributes equally to the making of the complete person. Furthermore, without this balance, gross distortion results. Both emotion and mind together constitute a balanced entity.

The redemptive purpose of God includes man's whole being, for the gospel creatively opens both the channels of the intellect and the emotions. The gospel affects everything that makes up a man. The Christian who is living the life of faith knows the gospel to be "good news for the *whole* man, not just for some department of his being or activity."[4] Life in Christ touches the furthest reaches of life.

The arts, too, address the whole man, requiring the integrated use of mind and emotion. They demand all of the human personality, both in making and in appreciating, for as noted by many philosophers and aestheticians, art speaks to mind and emotion simultaneously. Music in particular is a complex activity, each of its phenomena being related and balanced. Even music's two fundamental schools of aesthetic thought—the autonomous with its emphasis on reason (music has no meaning beyond its own intrinsic worth) and the heteronomous with its emphasis on emotion (the meaning of music is extra-musical) cannot stand alone. Each must be seen as a specific attempt to get at one side of the truth. They are correctives to each other. Charles Hoeffer notes that "it is nearly impossible for anyone to separate intellect and emotion when listening to music . . . " and that "composers don't write one piece to be heard intellectually and another emotionally."[5] Music is a unity and there can be no dividing it up:

> Music is not merely a succession of pleasing sound-patterns formed of sensuous tone; but is essentially an utterance of the whole man. Its message is not primarily addressed either to the intellect or to the emotions, but to the complete personality of the listener; and the message, to be valid, must spring from the complete personalities of both composer and performer.[6]

The life of faith, we have said, involves man's total being—intellect and emotion included. The arts (specifically music) speaking emotionally and intellectually, correspond beautifully with man's nature in this respect. Therefore, in order to get at the problem of a music that can strengthen and express the life of faith, we must further investigate the matter of religion and music as both intellectual and emotional.

There is an intellectual side to religion, though often it is mistrusted and thought of as either incidental or as a necessary evil. Particularly in evangelical Christianity, where emotion is considered primary, there are covert and sometimes overt moves to discredit the mind, although in the late sixties and seventies liberal theology, with its emphasis on celebration and the ecstatic, has moved toward a more visceral theology where feeling has become paramount. However, encounter with God is always accompanied by intellectual activity. Man must involve his mind in order to believe; without it he cannot come to God, or think of Him, or understand the Word, or communicate His love. If intellectual activity is omitted, even minimally, a distorted picture of God's revelation to man results. To repudiate mind and to concentrate on emotion is to relegate man to an existence as an unpredictable feeling vegetable. Christians cannot live this way in the faith.

Music, like religion, is very much an intellectual affair, but this view has many critics as well, particularly among those who see music as primarily emotive. The nineteenth-century musical commentator and aesthetician Edward Hanslick did noble battle with the advocates of the preponderant view of the day (i.e., that music creates in the listener pleasurable emotions and that these emotions are music's alpha and omega, the total reason for its being). In our own time, Stravinsky has emphasized the intellectual side of music. He believes that music has too long been subjected to the forcing of extra-musical associations upon it. For him, music is primarily an intellectual activity and its purpose is to be itself. He says:

> I consider that music is, by its very nature, powerless to *express* anything at all, whether a feeling, an attitude of mind, a psychological mood, a phenomenon of nature, etc. . . . . if, as is nearly always the case, music appears to express something, this is only an illusion, and not a reality.[7]

Paul Hindemith and Aaron Copland both emphasize music at the intellectual level, though neither would discount that music may be emotionally expressive. Hindemith believes that listening on the intellectual level is a matter of mentally reconstructing the inner workings of the musical components and that such an ability is necessary for full artistic appreciation of music. Copland thinks that listening on the musical (intellectual) plane is important enough to write a book about it, *What to Listen for in Music*. His book explains the component parts of music in a way that even the nonmusician can understand clearly and logically. "To listen intently, to listen consciously, to listen with one's whole intelligence is the least we can do in the furtherance of an art that is one of the glories of mankind."[8] One must listen with the mind in order to really hear, in order to perceive the "contours and inner lines, the lights and the shades, the rhythms and colors, and the constructional components."[9] The ear of reason is the basis of rational understanding.

It seems, then, that music is without question an intellectual activity, both in its creation and in its appreciation. The degree to which one emphasizes this activity depends upon individual orientation. For example, musicians and aestheticians, who are aware of formal beauty as a result of careful thought, are apt to accentuate mental activity. But we must realize that no musical composing, performing, or creative listening will take place without substantial use of the intellect. The composer-creator mind must be met by a listener-creator mind. Music, like faith, demands the use of reason.

The emotional side of religion has presented not nearly the difficulty for evangelical Christianity that the intellectual side has. "Giving one's heart to Christ" is a common subject for sermons. The well known bias for feeling is seen historically in the emphasis placed on emotion in the camp meeting, tent revival, and sawdust trail, as well as in the modern day phenomena of charismatic activity.

Man is a passionate creature and redemption involves all of man's being, including his emotions. His worship can be fervent, even impassioned, because he loves and feels deeply, realizing that the God he worships is a warm, understanding, divinely loving Person as evidenced in the giving of His Son Jesus Christ for man's salvation, in the record of Christ's dealings with man, and in man's personal experience and relationship with the Son of God. "In short, the divine as revealed in the Word can be an object of worship precisely because it can be the object of human emotion. And man can be an object of God's grace because he is an object of divine emotion."[10] The Bible emphasizes a warm, personal relationship between God and man by using anthropomorphic and anthropopathic words. But, the best representation of this relationship is Jesus Christ, who became man. According to the Biblical record, emotions are important, particularly in relation to man's heart as the seat of affective life, and are seen as needing redemption by virtue of being part of man's nature. Emotions form an important avenue of expression of praise and worship to the Creator. Human emotion cannot be neglected by religion. God is passionate, so through Christ He seeks passionate man.

"To believe" often implies dry intellectual assent to a religious proposition. But once belief becomes emotional, clothed in warmth, passion, and action, it becomes living faith and the life lived in faith knows well that the heart must be given its rightful place as that which energizes the intellect. Emotion is not to be shunned. It is the fire of the faith life.

The predilection on the part of some listeners to view music as a means of expressing emotion is the result of personal interpretation of one's own reaction in listening. This notion is widespread and the reinforcement afforded it by others who corroborate the view (that music is emotional expression) suggests that "music-emotion" must be taken seriously. Only a few disagree. Psychological tests have proved that music does influence man's affective state.

What one brings to the musical encounter by way of taste, background, age, interest, musical experience, and association, will in large measure determine the emotional quality of his response. To the degree that these items are similar, the response will likewise be similar. Studies of the affective responses of native West Africans to western (European) music show them to be markedly different from those in persons schooled in the western tradition. Even within a given culture there are too many variables to be able to predict with accuracy the specific emotional responses that a certain composition will produce. One cannot give specific emotional (or any other) meaning to music. However, because music cannot be specific does not suggest that it is emotionally short-changed. It can speak with depth and intensity, and it is precisely its subjectivity, its ability to speak individually, that is its strength. The feeling side of music is real, though it is nebulous, unpredictable, ethereal, ambiguous, and mystical. Music is emotional, but emotional in a musical way. Emotion is primary in the sense that it always accompanies music, but secondary in that it is inconsistent and mutable.

We have stated that religion and music each have an intellectual and an emotional side. Both contribute to the Christian faith as a mode of living by being part of the balance needed for holistic living. In church we should expect that expressions to and from the worshipper demonstrate that he is a whole being. Musical expression in worship must have an emotional and intellectual aspect because, as we have seen, that is the nature of man, the nature of music, and the nature of religion. At its best, music should demonstrate this life-religion-music unity in worship by a well-proportioned, reasoned, feeling approach to composition.

> If there is anything that should distinguish music in church from music anywhere else, it is not so much a peculiar style, as this unity holding in perfect balance the claims of our mind and our emotions.[11]

II. Intellectual and Emotional Imbalances in Church Music

To emphasize emotion at the expense of reason, or reason at the expense of emotion, is to produce music that is handicapped, even crippled, in its articulation to and from man. "Man is not a creature moved by reason on Monday, and emotion on Tuesday, but his reason is emotional and his emotions reasonable."[12] Yet often in worship we find a lack of balance in these two areas. Such imbalance in worship expression, edification, or witness is unhealthy because only one side of man's being is participating in what should essentially be an affair of the whole man.

Intellectually it is possible for church music to have this imbalance on two levels. First, the music itself is involved. We have said that the making of music is a matter of creative intuition and craftsmanship. Normally if music is weak it is because of poor technique rather than a lack of inspiration. However, music can be so contrived that it is deprived of its ability to speak emotionally. Technique alone does not make good church music. For example, there are those who feel that music in the French Ars Nova exhibits complexity for complexity's sake. Johannes Galiot (second half of the fourteenth century) was "too occupied with syncopation and cross-rhythms to produce music that is moving as well as technically proficient."[13] Jacopin Selesses has, in the opinion of Archibald T. Davison and Willi Apel, written music of such striking rhythmic complexity that it "has never been paralleled in all music history."[14] Albert Seay feels that in this historical period

> The interest already found in music as a technical toy became, by the end of the century in France, the overriding concern; we can only react, in all too many cases, with a certain amazement at the amount of sterile complexity and meaningless intricacy therein.[15]

Other examples of music that may be technically correct but emotionally barren are works such as study fugues written for the mastery of polyphonic compositional skill. Imogene Horsley believes such fugues to be "contrived models," which, though important as teaching devices, "should never be mistaken for musical reality."[16] James Higgs concurs:

> Probably the fugue thus made [as compositional exercise] will prove but a mechanical composition . . . the student must not mistake the means for the end, or think that, being able to analyse a composition or reproduce resemblances of its several parts or even an imitation of the whole, he is necessarily possessed of the power to produce a true and worthy work of art.[17]

Julius Portnoy notes that composers, under certain conditions, can create that which is "emotionally void, is highly refined, and full of technical stratagems."[18] Music requires something more than technique. To put notes down correctly, even brilliantly, without inspiration, a caring attitude, inner warmth, or passion woven into the very fiber of the art form, is to make music mechanistic. Such a music based on intellectualized writing only produces deformed church music and while this is not a major problem for the church musician, it is nevertheless important enough to be aware of it.

The second level of intellectual imbalance which may occur in a church music situation is caused by a lack of musical understanding on the part of the congregation. Hindemith shows that in order to apprehend music comprehensively there must be a certain amount of intellectual musical understanding on the part of the listener. He says, however, that because individuals vary greatly in their ability to reconstruct music mentally, music should have a certain balance between stringent and less stringent musical requirements: that is, between simpler construction (brief, symmetrical phrases, for example) and more complex constructions (such as longer, asymmetrical phrases).[19] Therefore, the level of difficulty used in the church depends upon the general musical ability of the congregation—not the ability to perform only, but the ability for rational understanding in listening. Hindemith also says that the musical structure should not be so alien that one has not the faintest idea of its probable movement.[20] He is not suggesting standardized music,[21] but is arguing for music which has one foot in tradition so that there can be some basis for the listener

> to conjecture with a high degree of probability its presumable course. A musical structure which due to its extreme novelty does not in the listener's mind summon up any recollections of former experiences, or which incessantly disappoints his constructive expectations, will prevent his creative cooperation.[22]

The grasping of music intellectually, which we have said accompanies full life in the faith, should be of major concern for the minister of music. Music must not be so intellectual that it is emotionally barren, and more important, the choice of music must take into account the musical capabilities of the congregation. The minister of music must know his congregation well enough to be able to plot carefully his musical program in such a way that the music will be grasped and at the same time serve as a stepping stone to new and greater things. If music is trite there is no challenge; if it is consistently too difficult, discouragement and bewilderment will set in. Intellectual listening will not take place, and the music ministry will be lopsided.

Even as the intellectual aspect of music may be stressed at the expense of emotion so the opposite is true. Usually, though, the emotional aspect is emphasized and the intellectual side is ignored. For example, the gospel song is emotional through and through with no concern for the intellectual qualities of music; Victorian hymnody and anthem literature have a strong inclination toward the cloying, sentimental, and sweet; much late nineteenth and early twentieth-century American church music consists of musical composition in which emotional effect is the *raison d'etre* of the genre; and the main feature of modern religious pop-gospel-rock is the exchange of substantial musical ideas and development for emotionalistic drive. Emotionalism in music is that which has as its primary function the stirring up of emotions. It gainfully employs proved patterns of sound for the manipulation of feeling—contrived, artifical, and planned. It is the "evocation or the seeking of emotional satisfaction divorced from reason . . ."[23] It is the calculated short-circuiting of deep and costly experience to produce enjoyment without personal involvement. Daydreams, fantasy, and escape rather than emotional reality and maturity are the characteristics of emotionalistic music. To renounce the intellect and concentrate on emotions is to destroy the integrity of the music. It becomes entertainment.

Entertainment is a word common to our society, but it has yet to be accepted as viable activity in worship, at least in name. Notice the phrase "in name," for in actuality, more entertainment is received in church services than one would dare admit. That is the problem—we do not recognize it in worship (the music director included) until it is too late, until a mind set has taken hold, until values and attitudes have hardened, and, sorry to say, until the Christian has been hooked.

To entertain (as we are using the word) is to amuse, to wile away the time in frivolous activity, to by-pass the mind, to make pleasure the end, to achieve one's goal without travail, to gratify one's need for diversion, to revert to a mindless entity where the emotions reign supreme. The predisposition toward dionysian enjoyment is the root of the problem. Our hedonistic society, in which self-pleasure is the chief good and priority (though unacknowledged), has so infiltrated the church that often it is impossible for the average church-goer to differentiate between good feelings and worship. When entertaining music (i.e., music that shortchanges the intellect) produces good feelings year after year, a music-entertainment-pleasure syndrome is set up by association. Like Pavlov's experiments in conditioning, there only needs to be the entertainment stimulus and one "worships;" no "proper" stimulus, no worship.

The problem with entertainment music is that emotionalism helps, even pushes, the worshipper toward becoming more and more self-centered, which is to say more infant-like, more selfish, and more egocentric than his already ample natural inclination evidences him to be. His insatiable desire for that which makes him feel good centers worship on the self—the pleasure-seeking self. Emotionalistic self-gratification becomes the unacknowledged purpose of worship.

Entertainment-induced and oriented worship is in fact idolatrous because man makes himself the center of his worship. He stimulates himself. In using emotionalistic music in worship, he is fed that which he has selfishly desired and made, which in turn whets his appetite for more of the same in an endless cycle. The extreme subjectivity produced as a result of overindulgence in this one-sided emotionalism shows God to be a mere tool in the satisfaction of man's craving for pleasure.

The minister of music, realizing the problems of music which is overintellectualized and emotionalistic, will be very careful in his selection of music. He must not choose material that is emotionally stacked or intellectually barren. The musician

> knows that music limited to the level of sense will result in the same satiety and eventual disgust which reward sensuality in any other area of life. He also realizes that music whose appeal is limited to the intellect will leave him and all others cold.[24]

To emphasize emotion over intellect, or intellect over emotion, is not to minister to the whole man. The life of faith demands that the music of the church both express and minister to man's total being. One-sidedness results in a deformed ministry and unbalanced Christians. Theologically, such art is false.

No person can be consistently fed that which is only intellectualized, clever, astute, brilliant, and ingenious, or only escapist, amusing, cloying, entertaining, standardized, uncreative, sensational, and trite, without somehow forming the idea that our faith is either identical with or expressed by one or the other of these qualities. Balanced church music offers modern man help in developing a more mature faith, both emotionally and intellectually. The church musician has a responsibility here that goes deeper than commonly acknowledged, for his music making can and must contribute significantly to his congregation's spiritual growth.

III. Faith Action and Tendency Gratification

The life of faith also calls us to a specific type of faith action. This type of faith involves stepping into the unknown, the unfamiliar, as though it were known and familiar. It is "the assurance of things hoped for, the conviction of things not seen."[25] Moreover, faith action cannot be reduced to the calculation of facts with a thus determined answer. In this respect faith is not reasonable. There is an unknown quality about it. On the other hand, it is not an illusion. Faith is a reasonable activity of man's life. Through faith we believe we will not be poisoned by our next meal; the alarm clock has awakened us before and will (we hope!) do so again. We do not "know" these things. The evidences, however, point to the fact that it is reasonable to eat as though we will not be poisoned and sleep as though we will be awakened. There is a paradox here. Christianity is not sheer logic, yet it tallies with experience. Trueblood believes "the most fundamental of all religious paradoxes is that of faith and reason."[26] To have faith there must be reason, and to have reason there must be faith.

The general sphere of Christian faith discussed in the first section (i.e., faith as a mode of being) now calls for a specific, positive, active faith. Active faith involves risk by venturing into the unknown with the confidence that it is reasonable to do so. Though one cannot see the end, the answer, or the outcome, one is to live creatively in freedom. To know the ending before beginning, to have the answer before asking, to know the outcome before trying, is to be safe, secure, inhibited, and ultimately bound. But the unknown should be within the normal state of existence for the Christian. He does not have to play it safe. Life in Christ is a risky adventure that leads home.

Church music as the expression of the Christian faith must align itself with its understanding of the faith. We have said that active faith entails risk. Such an attitude can be incorporated into the music of the church in two ways. First, faith action can be shown through the use of unfamiliar music in worship. A risk is taken in expressing the faith through the unknown because one is called upon to deal musically with uncertainty, puzzlement, and ambiguity. A music program that relies heavily on what people know or on certain closed styles is a repudiation of the meaning of faith. That which is well known eventually tends to become habitual, which is to say comfortable and familiar. The faith adventure, then, musically speaking, is replaced with reliance on security; yet it is theologically false to represent the Christian life as "one long rest in bed."[27]

To use music as a security blanket is dangerous. If Sunday after Sunday the musical fare is security-seeking music, then the equation will be made, either consciously or unconsciously on the congregation's part, that religion is comfortable. It is nice. One is soothed and finally anesthetized. The element of risk in going to the brink—which demands faith—will be denied. The Christian will return to the womb.

However, if the music director chooses music which is inscrutable in its newness (perhaps stylistically as well as specifically), the congregation will see the subject of that music, namely, Christianity or an aspect thereof, as that in which there is an unknown, in which faith must come into play. Hence one needs to deal with, in this case listen to, the unknown by welcoming its strangeness, realizing that not everything in life is within the Christian's control or immediate apprehension, and by exercising one's faith (through the faith action of creative listening) that *someone* (the composer or, theologically, God) is in control and knows what is going on. Faith will keep us from turning aside from the unfamiliar, the unexplored, and the hidden. The Christian sees and hears through the eyes and ears of faith.

The second way in which faith action can be shown in worship is through the principle of delayed gratification. Heinrich Schenker's theory that musical structure can be reduced to a simple shape defined by the musical goals (cadences)[28] of the composition puts the principle of delayed gratification in perspective. There is little musical worth to the bare outline. It is the process of reaching the cadential goals that contributes to and determines musical value and worth. The method of inhibiting, delaying, and resisting a direct and immediate approach to the musical dilemma (the need for musical resolution) gives the composition its artistic desirability. The skill of the composer is shown in his ability to creatively delay artistic consummation. Leonard Meyer points out:

> (1) that a melody of a work which establishes no tendencies, if such can be imagined, will from this point of view (and others are possible) be of no value. Of course, such tendencies need not be powerful at the outset, but may be developed during the course of musical progress. (2) If the most probable goal is reached in the most immediate and direct way, given the stylistic context, the musical event taken in itself will be of little value. And (3) if the goal is never reached or if the tendencies activated become dissipated in the press of over-elaborate or irrelevant diversions, then value will tend to be minimal.[29]

Goal-inhibiting processes or the concept of delayed gratification is to be seen as a means for establishing worth in music and also can be viewed as the musical analogue of faith action. That is to say, by faith one knows that the goal will be reached, but does not know the route to reaching that goal. The sovereign God has control and man in blind but responsible trust knows that the detours of life refine, cleanse, purge, purify, fashion, and shape him into something more valuable in God's eyes than he would be if life were only continuous bliss. To become a beautiful vessel one must first go through the painful experience of becoming malleable clay. The end cannot be reached without the process of becoming, and it is the becoming which is the unknown quantity. It is here that faith comes in. For faith to be active, there must be the willingness to experience creatively what one does not know, in the certain knowledge that he is being led rightly to the conclusion of the matter. Musically the church can show this theological concept of acting in faith as it affirms little known music that is mature, incorporating the musical gratification techniques characteristic of great art. The worshipper must hear with the attitude that ultimately he will understand (even minimally), but for the moment must be content to realize that he is moving in a musical time segment which he knows not but believes in.

The principle of delayed gratification, however, is anathema in contemporary culture. Our entire society is patterned after its exact opposite, the principle of immediate gratification. So pervasive is immediate gratification that it has spawned a whole series of modern day phenomena of the "do it now" species: "piano playing in ten easy lessons," "buy now, pay later," "electronics made simple," "witnessing in three easy steps," and items such as instant potatoes, number paintings, and literary condensations. Man is caught up in the immediacy of the moment without preparation or thought for the future. It is said that the most direct route to the gratification of one's desires is the best.

The church needs to do everything it can to counteract this tendency in its own life; after all, its eschatological orientation shows us that we are, in a sense, but pilgrims and sojourners who move forward to that sought-after goal of eternity with our Lord. The man of faith is not concerned with find-ing an answer now, because he knows there will be one. Through faith, he walks from one horizon to the next. The certainty of his reaching it frees him from trying to manipulate his course in order to obtain it now. The church, however, shows its naiveté, according to Herman Berlinski, when it ap-propriates music that has immediacy as its prime characterisitic (such as com-mercial pop) and uses it in worship. The Judeo-Christian tradition, violently opposed to the hedonistic principles which are the philosophic assumptions of such music, is the last place such music should fit.[30] Pop music's very neatly packaged novelty, its limited musical vision, its smug self-satisfaction, its lack of discipline and mature musical development, are qualities we would ex-pect the church to avoid in its music. Again, note Meyer's findings on this musical genre:

> The differentia between art music and primitive music lies in speed of tendency gratification. The primitive seeks almost immediate gratification for his tenden-cies whether these be biological or musical. Nor can he tolerate uncertainty. And it is because distant departures from the certainty and repose of the tonic note and lengthy delays in gratification are insufferable to him that the tonal reper-tory of the primitive is limited, not because he can't think of other tones. It is not his mentality that is limited, it is his maturity. Note, by the way, that popular music can be distinguished from real jazz on the same basis. For while "pop" music whether of the tin-pan-alley or the Ethelbert Nevin variety makes use of a fairly large repertory of tones, it operates with such conventional clichés that gratification is almost immediate and uncertainty is minimized.[31]

Immediate gratification, then, is antithetical to great value in music because it has poor goal-inhibiting tendencies, or in our terminology, no faith ac-tion. Music showing delayed gratification manifests maturity, discipline, restraint, and the faith action of believing that beyond the present uncer-tainty is the certainty of achieving the goal. The church needs to testify to its culture that all of life is more than momentary expediency.

Church music, exhibiting faith-action in musical terms, knows that its goal will be reached but does not know the route. It is this resistance to standard-ized patterns of musical development that not only determines its musical worth, but, in its being an analogue of faith-action, determines its theological worth. One ought to be constantly surprised, delighted, pained, shocked, unsettled, and wondering as the music moves steadily and unceasingly toward its inevitable final cadence. If the music attempts immediate gratification through poor syntactical grammar, not only will we have lesser art, but *the faith principle will be denied.* The satisfaction of the moment must be postponed so that greater depth and meaning of the whole will be advanced. We would expect that any work of art pregnant with meaning by virtue of its well-thought-through internal progression would have something to say, even upon repeated hearings, and would speak loudly and clearly that, as church music, here is faith in action.

Thus we view faith action first as that listening which eagerly welcomes unknown church music because such listening exercises musical-theological faith in keeping one from an addiction to the secure, the comfortable, and the familiar. Music in its representation of the Christian life as an adventure must show adventuresomeness within itself. Second, faith action is shown by that music which grants the listener little immediate satisfaction but requires the listener to participate in the musical working-through of the entire composition before any degree of musical fulfillment takes place. The detours in music and in life, when perceived through faith, can be seen as that action which produces greater value.

IV. Summary and Congregational Methodology

Faith, then, is an important ingredient in living a full Christian existence, entailing, as we have noted in this chapter, wholeness (the life in faith) and risk (faith action). The church music program ought to reflect the mature walk in Christ and provide sustenance, inspiration, and encouragement to its constituents. Such a program improves worship music, first of all, by doing away with the sacred-secular dichotomy and by balancing emotion and reason. Second, the program should omit security-seeking music thereby demonstrating that the deliberate developmental process of delayed musical gratification gives church music its value and is a musical analogue of faith. Any music that seeks to focus on the whole man, emotionally and intellectually, that causes him anguish as well as joy, and that does not judge its success on the basis of immediate gratification (in other words exhibits the faith principle) is the music that the Christian church must embrace. It is a music that witnesses to our faith and musically exercises our faith.

Much of what has been mentioned in the preceding pages needs to be explained to a congregation if a new direction in church music is to have meaning, particularly when past musical practice is markedly different from what is being attempted. The days of the church musician as silent partner in the religious enterprise are over. The tangled web of conflicting musical philosophy brought about in large measure by the variety of musical expressions available within our culture through all kinds of electronic media makes it absolutely mandatory for the church musician to become an articulate spokesman and teacher. It is his job to find ways to help the congregation understand the full implications of its musical life both by direct teaching and by new musical creativity. Such a venture can be an exciting partnership between clergy, laity, and musician in the faith pilgrimage of the collective people of God. It need not be a chore. The oft-experienced misunderstandings between musician and people will be greatly reduced by this joint effort in which choice of music is carefully explained in Biblical and theological terms. Then and only then will the creativity of God's people be unleashed openly and freely without reluctance, hesitation, or ill will. Expressing the full meaning of faith in a musical way will be a happy exercise dependent upon cooperative effort and full of promise and stimulating adventure.

7

STEWARDSHIP

I. Motivations for Stewardship

Usually Christian stewardship is given particular emphasis when there is to be a special financial drive of some kind, perhaps for the church budget, missionary program, new organ, building fund, or other projects. Full stewardship, though, involves much more than money. It also involves giving all of oneself (time, abilities, and money) with the understanding that these are a trust from a loving God to be used to the fullest for the upbuilding of the total kingdom. In effect, stewardship is God-oriented management—management of all that we are and have for the purpose of fulfilling God's plan for His creation, the church, and the individual.

The motivation for that management is important, for without right motivation, a person may come to rely (often unconsciously) on the good works of a sterling stewardship to "earn" his standing before God. Salvation, then, might very well be thought of as the result of good deeds rather than the gift of free grace. We find among the reformers a stewardship that produced great works that were motivated not by the need to earn salvation but by the need to evidence God's free salvation. Motivations such as expectation of reward, legalism, loyalty to organizations, and humanistic concerns, are unworthy because they are all based on reasons that are oriented around man, law, or self-interest rather than on God and His freely given salvation. In being redeemed, man knows himself to be freely responsible, accountable, and gently wooed into fuller commitment. Our motivation for stewardship, then, rests first on what God has done in Jesus Christ and on our having taken upon ourselves His name in full commitment.

Second, our motivation rests on the fact that God is literally the Creator and Owner of everything, and we as recipients and stewards of His gifts are utterly, completely, and finally dependent. There is literally nothing that we can do in and of ourselves, for whatever we are or become is a grant or trust from God. Our receivership of God's endowments puts us in a place of humility, which, when coupled with our own self-worth, becomes the church musician's basic pose. We are debtors, and as stewards, owe everything to our Lord.

Third, man made in God's image through Christ is unfinished even as creation is unfinished. In our use of the gifts God has given us, we are participating in the ongoing creation of ourselves and the world. We become co-creators with God in the *creatio continua* by allowing God to work through us as we fulfill our responsibility of being channels of His creativity. Each of us has both the ability and the duty to use his God-endowed talents in the service of Christ; each has the ability by virtue of his being made in God's image and the duty by virtue of being both a man and a Christian. He is free to sing, to dance, to think, to create, to be open to new possibilities. As a creator he cannot be stereotyped in his actions or thinking, and he cannot be made exempt from his responsibility of being a channel.

> Every person has the task of releasing angels by shaping and transfiguring the raw materials that lie about him so that they become houses and machinery and pictures and bridges. How we do this—how we "build the earth," to use Teilhard de Chardin's phrase—is determined by the discovery and the use of our gifts.[1]

Fourth, our motivation rests in the fact that the Creator is love and our only fitting response to God's love is to love Him in return as we are bound together with our fellow men. This was the foundation of Luther's ethical principle. Love is more than idealized circumspection for the highest good; love is that which causes you to give to your neighbor all you have, and it is in loving your neighbor that you love God. The love shown here is *agape* love, a self-giving love which asks for nothing in return and seeks no conquest or possession. *Agape* love "assumes an other-regarding style of expression which affirms the 'other' in his freedom, integrity, and uniqueness."[2] It is the love that God has shown to us in the gift of His only Son, the love that is the deepest reason for our being good stewards of all He has given us.

The motivation for stewardship, then, stems from the fact that: (1) God has redeemed us and we are His disciples; (2) we are debtors, for God is the owner and giver of all that we have; (3) we have been given the responsibility to use our gifts in God's full-orbed plan of ongoing creation; and (4) our response to God's love is the giving of our gifts in *agape* love. Stewardship does not come from our ingenuity but from Christ's power as we allow Him to work in us.

II. Stewardship's Scope

In addition to understanding the reasons and motivations behind stewardship, we need to discover the parameters of stewardship in greater detail. The view we have taken is that the spiritual and material aspects of life are a unity, and that stewardship involves all of it. Man as a unified being is called to think in terms of the totality of his being. Stewardly creativity is not solely for the spiritual side or the material side, for such dichotomy for the Christian is a false one. Karl Rahner questions:

> And why should not the workman, indeed any man who makes the world into what it ought to be, see the exercise of his creative powers as a sharing in that New Creation wrought in the life and death of Him who makes all things new?[3]

In being faithful, one gives everything to God, not only for the immediate good, but as a symbol of the deeper meaning of an obedient discipleship. The narrow sense of religion as prayer and praise is only a part of man's religious life and needs to be joined with the creative action of everyday living. The concept of the stewardship of life as a whole manifests itself every second of the day, bringing one to the conclusion that good stewardship from Monday through Saturday is as important as good stewardship on Sunday. It is this consistency that gives worship and the whole Christian life credibility.

In the larger sense, a believer's "vocation" is always to be Christian. To put it another way, for the Christian, any job is full-time Christian service. In daily life, toil becomes holy as he responds to God through his work. The glory of God is shown through a right use of the gifts He has given.

In his book, *My Job and My Faith,* Frederick K. Wentz, President of Hamma School of Theology at Wittenberg University, includes twelve essays by laymen on the interrelation between their faith and their work. In summing up these essays, Dr. Wentz concludes that there are significant theological themes present in what he terms "lay theology," that are "the coherent interpretation of their lifestyle [sic] which laymen develop from their own experiences in a gospel-world encounter."[4] Several themes are common throughout: creation—God, as Creator, has made and is making the world and is therefore active in business or wherever one works; stewardship—one uses his talents to participate in creation; vocation—the oneness of the Christian and the "vocational" life.[5]

The church musician needs to participate fully in such a theology: that the Creator is continuing to create; that God calls him to continue creation through his music making; and, that music and religion are interrelated. Yet music in the church is often relegated to a state of low creativity because it is not important enough to be taken seriously as a way of glorifying the Creator. As a vocation it is seen not as a unification of religion and art, but as two separate worlds—one higher (spiritual) and one lower (musical). The Christian musician is often called upon, in the name of religion, to reject his stewardship of God's gift of music by creating music of such poor quality that it degrades the creative gift. Theology that concerns itself with "spiritual matters" as opposed to and over "worldly matters" will always treat art as a frivolous endeavor. This attitude is seen in John Ruskin's *Stones of Venice*: "I never yet met with a Christian whose heart was thoroughly set upon the world to come, and, so far as human judgment could pronounce, perfect and right before God who cared about art at all."[6] Such a position is one that is all too common. If life is a oneness between "religion" and "music," for example, let not the church muddy the waters by asking the musician to renounce one for the other. Authentic Christianity repudiates dualistic religiosity wherein the Christian composer is required to reject his creative integrity when composing "religious" music and to use his best creative integrity when composing for the "world." Such a dualism is erroneous.

III. Doing One's Best — Principle One

The concept of stewardship has two important principles that must not be neglected by the church musician in his quest for a philosophical premise from which to work. We will thoroughly investigate the parable of the talents to discover these two interrelated stewardship principles so necessary for the pastoral ministry of music: (1) doing one's best, and (2) the growth principle.

The parable is Jesus' most characteristic method of teaching. It is a literary form akin to the fable but taken from the familiar areas of common life. To understand properly what Jesus has to say through this literary genre, the parable must be seen as genuine art form and, as such, creative imagination is necessary in getting to the parable's intent. One must go beyond the apparent meaning of the words of the text to get to the implicit truth of the parable.

> For the kingdom of heaven is as a man travelling into a far country, who called his own servants, and delivered unto them his goods. And unto one he gave five talents, to another, two, and to another, one; to every man according to his several ability; and straightway took his journey. Then he that had received the five talents went and traded with the same, and made them five other talents. And likewise he that had received two, he also gained other two. But he that had received one went and digged in the earth, and hid his lord's money. After a long time the lord of those servants cometh, and reckoneth with them. (Matthew 25:14-19 KJV).

The parable begins by stating that each man was entrusted with that which was not his own but which belonged to the master. This is quite in line with what we have said both about creation and about stewardship. Everything is from God. Moreover, no one is without a gift. All of us have received something useful for the upbuilding of the Kingdom—among them the gift of music, either as composer, performer, or listener. However, the parable refutes the idea of equality of gifts. The stewards had nothing to say about what they received. God in His own sovereign wisdom determined what each one should receive. Such a realization should cause one to accept himself and his gifts, whatever they are, with thanks. There are those with greater gifts and some with lesser ones. Whatever the gift, one must be faithful to use it. The accounting which took place was concerned with what each did with what was received, because faithfulness is the measure of God's accounting.[7]

The commendation the faithful servants received from their lord was given because each man had done his best with what had been given him. The phrase "doing one's best" is, no doubt, overworked. It is usually used as an excuse for mediocrity or to indicate an effort that was unadmittedly halfhearted because great care and concern were lacking. However, the principle of "doing one's best" is pregnant with meaning. God does not call for a specific level of achievement measured by objective analysis. Rather, the Lord is concerned that what each does is the ultimate of that of which he is capable. This is the sole measure of God's evaluation of a man's work. Failing to fulfill his capabilities is sacrilege.

Faithful stewardship, utilizing to the maximum the gifts each possesses, is the measure of success which should concern a musician in the pastoral ministry. We are called to develop and to give the best of what we have. Johann Sebastian Bach, a composer who in all his work brought his native talent to its highest possible development in the service of the church, was such a church musician. The musical talents we have received from God are not exempt from stewardship. A musician is "called" just as a "Christian teacher, minister, scholar, merchant, housewife, or anybody else . . . has been called by the Lord to specific work in line with his or her talents."[8] The musician will answer for that which has been entrusted to him. For example, when a composer (or performer or listener) is content with poor work, yet is capable of better, he shows poor stewardship.

> The awkward harmonization, the poorly worked-out counterpoint, the nebulous formal structure . . . are let pass. Who will know the difference? What difference does it actually make? Content with slipshod work, the composer fails to provide the honest craftsmanship which a proper stewardship of his gift of the spirit demands.[9]

The musician then is called to give the best he has which, though never objectively good enough for God, is acceptable as the just fruit of his ability.

IV. Some Dangers

The parable of the talents gives an overall perspective to the minister of music. Objective musical standards, which are often lacking in our churches, must be seen in the light of the parable. Likewise, subjective standards must also come under the parable's scrutiny.

The parable warns the objectivist that artistic merit is not the sole criterion for music in the church. A music program that maximizes the talent and resources of a congregation, whatever its objective standards might be, is superior in God's eyes to the music program that does not. "Poor" may count for much more from a less musically competent congregation that is fulfilling its potential than "better" music does from a congregation that is slothful and could do more than it is doing. The church musician knows that in the final analysis what counts is not the artistic worth of the composition he does, but the worth of his people's strivings.

There are several dangers in the principle that "doing one's best" is all that counts, for it can become an excuse for sloth. People who think they are doing the best they can often are not. This is true, for example, regarding regular attendance by volunteers who staff the various choir ensembles, church school music programs, or instrumental groups. One's "best" might very well mean, "I'll come to rehearsal if I have nothing else to do." The thinking is that good stewardship is simply "being there when convenient." Obviously there is more to it than that.

Musicians are also to exercise right attitudes in stewardship. Singing with a begrudging or half-hearted spirit is dishonoring to the Lord, negating both one's discipleship and one's stewardship. Those few moments in rehearsal are precious and must be used wholeheartedly, and no one, director included, has the right to wile away the time unproductively for any reason. The Christian should treat each song and anthem as though it were his last, a final gift sung from a cheerful heart as tribute to the King of kings. One does not bring to worship a "consecrated" vehicle of praise which is ill prepared. Christian stewardship of the gift of music requires enthusiasm, discipline, and dedication. It requires on the director's part a mature understanding of people's musical abilities and the expectation that they can and will use them to their fullest, and on his choir's part the knowledge that doing their best will often require full participation when they do not especially feel like it. "Doing one's best" is a matter of the spirit.

There is a tendency for the expression "I'm doing the best I can" to have a negative connotation. It is often an excuse for not doing more (quantitatively) or not doing better (qualitatively). From a Biblical perspective, he who has done all that he possibly can has lived up to the highest standards—standards not of man but of God. Even as the Lord allows no temptation above that with which we are able to cope, so He asks nothing of us except as He supplies the grace and ability to accomplish it. It is, as it were, a tug of war between law and grace—law on the one hand demanding certain artistic dues that are good and right based upon universal artistic principles, and grace on the other, simply asking for our all—and that's it.

But more needs to be said. Daily living often shows us to be creatures who seldom come up to our full capabilities. That is the irony of it. We say that God expects our best, but psychologists state that in general, we use only about 10%-20% of our natural intellectual ability. Pastors complain that people are too busy for church but have plenty of time for their own activities. The financial stewardship campaign may be struggling, but as a nation we spend more on alcohol and tobacco than on the needs of the church. If humanity errs it is in the direction of not doing enough. We are still fallen.

When the music has been prepared as well as it can be, given the allotted time and abilities, the music director must assure the choir (and especially the nervous soloist) that since they have done their part as well as possible in preparation, the performance is now out of their hands. They should rejoice in the gift of using developed talents to their fullest—whatever they might be—not because of what man will think, but *because they know they have already pleased the Father.* The consecration of preparation is more important than the public performance. It is not the crowd's reaction that counts, but the performer's standing before God, stripped of everything (save an anointed stewardship).

Another great danger in the common usage of the phrase "doing one's best" is that the director of music will see "the best" as a reflection of something besides actual ability, more often a reflection of some type of conditioning. In church music, the congregation's "best" is often determined by what they are exposed to. Though sincere, hardworking, and dedicated, if the director is incompetent and influences the whole congregation toward mediocrity, then the best he knows will become the best they know. It is therefore incorrect to assume that they are really doing their best when actually they are only mirroring another's best. This problem broadens out to include a whole host of things, including the particular style of music, the difficulty of music (complexity is not necessarily good and simplicity is not necessarily bad), particular composers, a mind-set toward church "pop," or whatever. The result is a musical subculture which, for various reasons, imposes its definition of "best" upon a congregation. Obviously everyone is limited by the broader culture in some way, but for a congregation's musical level to be determined by a minuscule part of the general culture, thereby limiting creative vision, is to guarantee absolutely that Biblically-oriented stewardship will be drastically shortchanged.

The essential point, then, is that a minister of music ask from his people their very best, taking into account their natural ability, their training, and to a certain extent, their cultural environment. To ask for more than they can give is to ask too much, but to ask too little is Biblically reprehensible. The minister of music is a leader of stewards who must fulfill the broad call of God within the gospel framework.

Because of his high concern for Christian stewardship, every church musician worth his salt wants his ensemble to perform well. Yet often in volunteer situations, the end product of hours and hours of laborious rehearsal is so musically inferior in the eyes of the music director that he becomes mentally if not physically fatigued, and even sick, working himself into an extreme state of tension, nervousness, and anxiety. Here the parable shows, however, that he must be content with those people gifts God gives him and not covet and complain about being "shortchanged" (e.g., we have no tenors!). In other words, he is not to be ashamed of the fruit of the choir's labors when the choir has done its absolute best. Both level of difficulty and value of performance must be seen in the light of its strivings. The great temptation is for the music director to use music that is often too difficult for the choir, but because others do it, or because he knows it is good, or because he is expected to do it, he will make an attempt and in the process get himself and often the choir tied up in knots. This is quite unnecessary if he will: (1) use music the choir can handle (educationally there is much to be said on this subject), and (2) be really contented down deep with having the presentation prepared the best it can be under the circumstances, rather than placing one's contentedness in the group's ability to meet certain musical performance criteria. It is their best which ought to make the director of music feel fulfilled—not the artistic worth of their musical rendition.

All are stewards of God's gifts and are answerable to God for their use. The first stewardship principle is that God never requires more than that which people are capable of. He is just in His giving and receiving. He requires only our best.

V. Growth — Principle Two

The parable of the talents indicates that growth, our second stewardship principle, is necessary for healthy Biblical stewardship. The two profitable servants returned an increase to their lord. The two-talent servant brought four, and the five-talent servant brought ten. Stewardship of one's life includes the growth and multiplication of those raw materials that every man has been given at birth. God intends that man never stand still; to grow and live constantly in new discovery as we pilgrimage through time is part of the stewardship of our gifts. Maturing is becoming aware that life in God ever encompasses more and more of life. Heinrich Bornkamm has forcibly set forth this idea in his book, *The Heart of Reformation Faith.* Life is a journey, a process, a becoming. One is not fullgrown at birth. Furthermore, he quotes Luther who said: "This life is not being devout, but becoming devout, not being whole, but becoming whole . . . not a rest, but an exercise. We are not yet, but we shall be. It is not the end, but the way."[10]

Growth comes through some form of education (in the broadest sense), through formal study, observation, revelation, or experience, and is a matter of movement or change from one state to another, a never-ending activity. Life is one continual stream of change and stewardship encompasses all of it. The care and responsibility one shows in his growth entails every part of his existence, his vocation being creativity in the fullest sense. God has given man abilities and expects in return that they will have been expanded and multiplied, because stewardship means growth. Man is, in a sense, the tender of a garden.

Music, as a pervasive activity of life both without and within the church, is not excused from right stewardship. It is an activity found in all civilizations which often surpasses other cultural manifestations, and though not a particularly large part of the average parishioner's life in the sense of its being his profession, he does encounter music no matter where he goes. Even in worship we find that 30% to 50% of service time is normally taken up by it. We thus conclude that full stewardship of life must include growth in music. We cannot take such a matter lightly, for at stake here is more than music; that is, a church which promotes musical infantilism, soothing and placating the congregation rather than encouraging, even expecting, musical growth is ultimately at fault theologically. By its lack of concern for the musical stewardship of its congregation the church shows its unconcern for the teaching of our Lord in impacting the full dimension of life.

One of God's gifts to all men is the capacity to appreciate music, although the gift varies from individual to individual as other gifts do. Nevertheless, one usually possesses some inherent musical ability, and as a steward, man must seek to grow in his musical understanding and appreciation. "Of course, the ability to [fully] appreciate a work of art is not ready-made in most people: they have to be educated according to their capacity. But this is true for all intellectual activity."[11]

Musicians have a specific responsibility to the congregation for fostering growth in the understanding of music because without growth the musical ministry will stagnate, ultimately leading to a diminished stewardship, not only of music, but other areas of life as well. The die cast in the direction of perpetuating the status quo stamps an aura of stunted growth if not outright repression on the entire musical program. It then becomes a babysitting device, an entertainment accessory, a method of insuring that the Christian walk find its expression forever in terms of musical milk. Even as the child who stays in kindergarten his entire educational career will more than likely never develop his full potential, so the church-goer who sees worship music locked into his own peculiar and self-centered orientation will not find, musically speaking, the fullness of the Christian life. Many churches have not taken seriously this matter of training for musical growth. They often not only inadequately train but even actively undo the level of music appreciation and skill acquired in high school or private lessons by simply and implicitly equating poorer music with religion. They never attempt or even tolerate the suggestion to do anything better.

However, congregations can grow in musical taste as they are carefully nourished, their growth manifesting itself in a deeper and more meaningful worship of God as well as in a more viable Christian witness. Both director and congregation should feel a responsibility for promoting musical maturity. It cannot all be left to the pastoral ministry to initiate, prepare, and then force-feed the congregation. The people of God need some degree of eagerness to learn. Careful thought needs to be given especially to the music program for children because the musical and poetic standards of one's youth are the formative ones. Luther said:

> I am not of the opinion that because of the Gospel all arts should be rejected violently and vanish, as is desired by the heterodox, but I desire that all arts, particularly music, be employed in the service of Him who has given and created them. Unfortunately the world has become lax toward the real needs of its youth and has forgotten to train and educate its sons and daughters along proper lines. The welfare of our youth should be our chief concern.[12]

From a technical standpoint, then, the entire musical program needs to be built around the concept of music education. This is not to suggest that the church music program be thought of as just a music appreciation tool— that music and beauty are primary and the reason we educate is so we can better appreciate the artistic merits of great music for the sake of the music.

A Biblical philosophy of church music has a much different perspective. First, musical appreciation is relative to a congregation's abilities. High artistic merit or low artistic merit is not the scale of value. Second, the church should be concerned with musical growth as stewards who are called to cultivate and multiply God's gift. Thus the reason for appreciation in the church is not music or the self, but *to better honor and glorify the Creator who will call for an accounting of these gifts.* A Christian may appear from a distance to be an aesthete, but close examination should reveal him to be, as Derek Kidner puts it, an athlete.[13]

An athlete develops as he performs more and more difficult tasks related to his specific sport. Muscles are called upon to do what they are incapable of doing, and in the constant attempts they develop new levels of strength and dexterity. Higher standards are then set and the cycle begins again. Music that is easy and familiar is not a stimulant to musical growth. The congregation needs to flex its musical muscles in order to grow, to overcome the difficulties set before it, and to reach for a plateau of understanding from which the cycle can begin again.

Often the judgment pronounced on poorer hymns, for example, is unheeded by a congregation because of their attachment to them based on past use. For the Christian, what takes place in church is often the most cherished memory he has, because it is in the church that his life has taken on new meaning. The new convert or the growing child absorbs the music within that particular context, associates it and equates it with his spiritual experience. It is here that "Church music in particular is susceptible to sentimental attachment or memories, leading us to suspend taste when recollection of non-musical events is invoked."[14] Such psychological holds are very real and make growth in music difficult. But one of the marks of a Christian should be a teachable spirit. Understanding this, a congregation should be willing to give better music a hearing and to do away with the dross.

Lack of both familiarity and pleasant experiences, difficulty of language, and absence of a firm resolve have often made artistic music and especially twentieth-century music hard to incorporate consistently into a church's musical life. As we exercise our musical capabilities doing that which is difficult and that which requires real exertion to comprehend, we become musically athletic. For example, it is clear that

> contemporary music demands an active and often extensive effort from the listener. It is not easy music in any sense of the word. The passive listener, with dulled eardrums (a condition all too prevalent in this day and age), will *never* appreciate contemporary music.[15]

Contemporary church music of worth should be a common mode of musical expression in our time, but we must realize that a consistent program to expand a congregation's musical horizons is a necessity if this type of music is to have a positive hearing. This goes for any unfamiliar music of worth. Education is a must. We need to provide the stimulation and environment in which theological insights can be demonstrated in terms of both old and *new* melodies, harmonies, and rhythms—the sound of our twentieth-century creativity.

The task of music education requires a ministry of music which is capable of skill, ingenuity, openness, patience, and maturity. The saying, "start where the people are," is sound. The problem is that often one stays there too long! To "start where the people are" has become, practically speaking, "stay where the people are."

Growth in the level of musical appreciation can take place in any congregation blessed with an ordered, structured, coherent, and comprehensive music education program. It may be a slow process, but it can be done.

VI. Church Music Education

Specific details for the musical education of a congregation will depend upon the congregation's cultural background, native intelligence, church affiliation, attitude and interest; however, there are two general ways that music education can take place. The more obvious is a direct frontal assault on the problem by technical training of some sort. This is a natural method for graded choir programs, including adult choirs, and music organizations such as orchestras, bands, bell choirs, recorder groups, and the like. It is also possible for entire congregations to receive limited training before the worship service for specific projects, such as a congregational concertato, a new hymn, chorus, or service music. However, wide-scale technical training for the bulk of the congregation in such a setting is no doubt impractical.

A second approach to congregational music education is a consistent diet of music that will tend to maximize their musical resources, yet not be so difficult that it will alienate them. One need not lament a lack of formal musical training on the part of the congregation, because they who have never taken a music lesson in their lives may be more appreciative of great music than others who have had formal training. When one has an open attitude, consistent exposure to good music can raise the level of appreciation tremendously. The emphasis here is on doing rather than talking, on "active" listening rather than "passive" listening. It requires that one "sit quietly, and with every bit of mental energy you possess concentrate entirely on the music. This will not be easy at first. In fact, listening can be just as tiring as any other mental activity."[16]

The minister of music must recognize in his duty as musical educator that valuing and liking are two different things. He needs to stress that valuing is more important than liking and that a church music program can never be predicated upon liking alone. Yet as mastery develops in the growth process of valuing that which is "known" to be good, he can rest assured that the "affective" or emotional state characteristic of liking will ultimately appear.

The concept of stewardship can set the whole music program in perspective. There are situations where programming a steady diet of Bach, Byrd, Pinkham, Mozart, Victoria, Kodaly, Brahms, Mendelssohn, Barber, and Vaughan Williams would not only fail to do the job of increasing people's appreciation but actually so alienate them that there would never be a chance for new music to receive a fair hearing. One must not feel that every church must reach the level of Bach, Byrd, and Pinkham. The church which practices this repertoire may be just as guilty of poor stewardship as the church which is smugly satisfied with John Stainer, Ira Sankey, John Peterson, and William Gaither. Although God does not set up man-made levels of achievement to rate us by, He is concerned that we do our best *and* that we show growth within the hereditary and environmental framework in which He has placed us. There is no place for static musical indulgence.

A third approach to music appreciation in church is to set up times either in service, as a special mid-week study, or during church school when a Biblical perspective on church music can be spelled out. It is too much to expect that church-goers automatically understand everything that goes on in the music of the church simply because it takes place. Biblical teaching is as important to their musical growth stewardship as to any other area of life. The only way a congregation will understand why the music director does what he does, is for him to explain it to them. And if the director has good reasons, based on Biblical principles, the church music program should make progress. Not that this is the cure-all, for one cannot force-feed a person musical appreciation, but it is a beginning for him to know that the music has been deeply thought about, prayed over, and tested by the Word of God. Only then will the congregation begin to realize that there is more to music ministry than hitherto assumed. Let the musician become a teacher!

The church musician who works within stewardship guidelines will be in a much better position to minister to his people than one who forces arbitrary standards on them. His satisfaction is in the growth that music represents, rather than in doing particular music. If a church sings Bach chorales or nineteenth-century gospel songs, these are only bases from which to begin. In growing, the congregation witnesses to the gospel imperative of yielding a return on the investment God has made in His children.

VII. A Contrapuntal Stewardship

One must recognize danger in a philosophy of music that leans too heavily on one or the other of the two stewardship principles: (1) doing one's best, and (2) growth. On the one hand, there is the danger of a complete subjectivism, in which no objective standards are ever included in the music program. The ultra-pragmatist uses only music that works, music that is successful, music that does what he wants it to. For him that music is ''the best.'' Being a pragmatist, he is unconcerned that the music ever come under any objective authority, thereby effectively shutting himself and the entire music ministry away in a tight cocoon of subjectivity. However, to treat his ''best'' as a locked-in musical level is to misunderstand Christ's parable, because he is completely overlooking the second principle—growth.

On the other hand, being concerned only with the growth principle emphasizes an objectivity that produces the psychological warfare mentioned earlier. No matter how hard one tries, it is not good enough; the satisfaction of a job well done is gone because one cannot accept himself or his musical-church situation. One becomes dissatisfied, disillusioned, even bitter, as high hopes and grand visions are dashed to the ground because of the realities of an individual's or a choir's musical ability. The tendency might well be to give up and quit trying. We need objective criteria in the church to measure musical growth, but an objective standard must be a guide, not a slavemaster.

These two stewardship principles can only be useful in mutual association—a working contrapuntal relationship, if you will. Principle one (doing the best that you can) leans toward a subjectivity that is musically passive but is a necessary counterpoint for the objectivist who is largely concerned with artistry. On the other hand, principle two (growth) leans toward an objectivity that is musically aggressive and is a necessary counterpoint for the subjectivist who is concerned with maintaining the congregation's status quo.

The high calling of being a steward in the musical vineyard requires that we and our congregations (1) do the very best that we can in church music-making, and (2) foster a far-reaching music education program that causes us to grow as we exercise our native musical talents. Music is a useful tool in God's grand design of making us be what He wants.

Our satisfaction comes as a result of believing deeply that God is concerned with the strivings of his people. Naturally there will be musical rewards. But greater is the "pastoral" reward of seeing one's musical ensembles through the eyes of a loving father—a father who cares more that his three-year old loves him enough to make him a birthday card (resplendent in all its imperfections) than that the quality of the artwork on the card is inferior by "accepted standards." It is the motivation behind the deed that defines the loving act. The pastoral musician under the influence of these stewardship principles sees a deeper meaning to music than just the notes. He knows that God looks on the heart.

8

MYSTERY AND AWE

I. Music and Mystery

The omnipotent, omniscient, omnipresent, transcendent God who receives man's most personal and heartfelt worship and with whom he has a personal relationship is a mystery that man cannot fathom. God's otherness, His unknowableness, His hiddenness, His mystery, and the awe which grips man in truly contemplating the Holy, are important considerations both in understanding who He is and in assisting in forming a proper perspective of one's standing before Him. Indeed, some of the most important insights one can have of God are of His distinctiveness from man and the material world and His absolute unknowability in that "we know nothing of Him except what He Himself has revealed to us."[1] God is so exalted and so above man's comprehension that we must confess that whatever man can possibly imagine Him to be, He is infinitely more. Luther suggests:

> Nothing is so small but God is still smaller,
> nothing is so large but God is still larger,
> nothing is so short but God is still shorter,
> nothing is so long but God is still longer,
> nothing is so broad but God is still broader,
> nothing is so narrow but God is still narrower.[2]

God is in fact not to be thought of as an infinitely higher entity than man, for He is absolutely outside the scope of man's existence. God is not so much a mystery as He is mystery. Brunner contends that the mystery here is not similar to a riddle, because that would suggest that there may be a solution that will explain the enigma. But there is no solution to the mystery that is God. Men speak of Him as men who grope, who see through a glass darkly, who have not the slightest ability to unravel God's incomprehensibility, who cannot even remotely understand His inaccessibility and His transcendency. Simply put, God is Divine Mystery.

God is not only mystery, He is holy. Man speaks of holiness as a quality of life. One is holy only as he is holy unto God. Therefore, the quality of holiness as the term is commonly used is a derived one. But the holiness of God Himself is not a quality or even an attribute as much as it is a definition of God. It is that elemental ground which permeates the very nature of His Being. It separates the Creator from the created, the Incorruptible from the corrupt, the Pure from the impure. God alone can be holy. He is the Holy One.

The classic work which explores and develops this theme is Rudolf Otto's *The Idea of the Holy*. His thought revolves around the numinous, the state of being experienced by contact with the *mysterium tremendum* of the Holy. This contemplation of the Holy as felt in the numinous is one of dread, of being overpowered, of dynamic activity, of being struck dumb, of being both attracted to and simultaneously repelled by the "awefulness" of God. Man is shaken to the core at being confronted with the eternal mystery of God's holiness. Dwelling in "light unapproachable" man cannot look upon Him except indirectly and is even then overcome completely, being filled with fear and trembling, wanting to run away yet being attracted—*the mysterium tremendum et fascinans.*

The mystery of God and the awe one experiences in contemplating the Holy are important facets of Biblical truth that need to be known by every believer, for not only do they help in his understanding of God and his place before Him, but they aid in understanding his relationships with his neighbors. As Heinrich Bornkamm says: "this knowledge of the mystery of God, which is beyond us, is the deepest thing which binds us together as men, indeed, that which really makes us humans in the first place."[3] Not that we can fathom the depths of God's mystery and its meaning for us as men by erecting logical thought systems that enclose God in a man-sized parameter, for all such attempts are doomed to failure. But we need to make an effort to deal with these eternal mysteries which are beyond us, and in the trying, discover some of the reality of God's transcendence.

Even as we attempt to speak of God's mystery and holiness, we are incapable of understanding it. We also have the problem of attempting to communicate something through the medium of language about a God who cannot be bound by anything, including language. Our attempts become mere stammerings because language's very precision and excellence for making propositional statements is a limiting factor in helping man to really feel and know the inexplicable. The concepts of mystery and awe are so far removed from language's ability to say what really needs to be felt as well as known, that man is often tempted to give up in despair and avoid the whole business. But without a proper perspective of the transcendence of God, radical immanence often results. God becomes an over-familiar buddy and bosom pal.

The arts can help in this dilemma, for they have an immediacy, a feeling tone, and a drive that words do not possess. They can add significantly to our understanding of the truth of God, for "on the most subtle levels of religious thought words become clumsy; and we turn to the great artists."[4] That music has an important role in helping man to comprehend incomprehensible mysteries may be a surprise to many musicians, for we have normally thought theology to be a matter of words, including the words of our church music. However,

> Theology expresses itself not only in language, which is the chief medium of the professional theologian. Theology expresses itself also in the material forms which are the medium of the visual arts, including architecture, and in the audible forms which are the medium of the musician.[5]

If the pastoral ministry of music is to help men know a little more of the fullness of God, it must see its musical proclamation in such a theological and prophetic light.

Music strives toward making mysteries known through the artistic exploration of time and sound. All great art reveals a little bit more about the mystery and wonder of our world, which in turn shows more and more of the nature of the Creator of these elements, whether or not this is a stated objective of the artist. The space art of painting has more difficulty than the time art of music in expressing this quality of mystery because usually being representational, it becomes locked into known realities. The artist, then, must deliberately distort or "interpret" his subject in some way in order that the mystery of what he sees, which is hidden from everyone but himself, may be made known. Abstract impressionism, in freeing painting from precise meanings, is better equipped to deal with mystery than the nineteenth-century landscape painters, for example, because of the latter's literal representation of the world. Biganess Livingstone, a twentieth-century painter, was commissioned to do a major painting suggesting the theme implicit in the title of the chapel of Granwell School for Boys, "The Chapel of the Servant." She began with a literal depiction of Christ washing the feet of one of the disciples, but realizing that over the years and upon repeated viewings it would not convey the awe and mystery implicit in the theme, she did five more versions. Each version progressively moved from literalism to more abstraction and stylization until she felt she had captured the inner essence of her subject. She knew that the mystery of it would not be able to be dissipated by complete or immediate apprehension. In her movement toward abstractness, her painting became less representational and more "musical."

The abstract quality of music, its ambiguity, is its strength. Music does not have specific meaning but it does have meaning. It is this ethereal quality of tones moving fleetingly in time, heard but never touched, tasted, seen, or smelled that makes music the most logical of all the arts to deal with mystery. Music orders sounds or combinations of tones in a time frame, only a fraction of which can be heard at any given instant. It is music's constant moving and shifting, its never standing still long enough for leisurely examination that leaves us moved and stirred to our depths for unknown reasons. The creative use of music's ephemeral nature, then, is a large part of its ability to deal in mystery—an ability that meets one of our deep needs.

> The other arts, though highly inspirational, are not as mysterious as music; for music is something you cannot see, you can only hear it and feel its impact. I believe it was Plato who said, "Music is to the mind what air is to the body."[6]

It is possible to write music that is not equipped to explore mystery and engender awe. When it is composed in such a manner that everything is expected, known, and cozily comfortable, when stereotyped rhythms, melodies, and harmonies are blended into conventional banality, or when predetermined formulas or artistic gimmicks are used instead of fresh creativity, there is in the lessening of the artistic quality a lessening of its ability to explore mystery. Stock standardization is hardly mysterious. When music's whole thrust is toward that which can be known as simply, as immediately, as easily as possible, it does not have a prophetic concern for the mystery of the eternal.

II. Truth and Musical Composition

We have said that music's abstractness is one of the qualities that gives it a natural propensity for the mysterious. But it is not only isolated abstract sound such as a chord or two on the piano that contributes to its mysterious capability; it is, as we have suggested, the integrity of the total art form that brings the mysterious quality of music into the realm of meaning—significant meaning for mankind. Why significant? Because there are many peripheral meanings that can be assigned (such as literary, pictoral, sensuous, and emotive meanings), each of which must be set aside if music is to be described in a way that corresponds to its innermost nature. Ultimately it is truth that comes to be seen as one of the major meanings of music. We do not here use "truth" in the factual sense, as is the case of mathematical, theological, or philosophical propositions, but truth in the sense of rightness—a rightness that is correlative with all that is already known of God in His creation.

When we are startled with the notion that the subject of music's mystery is truth, the inevitable questions that arise are to be expected, for is not truth a matter of tightly knit, absolutely irrevocable, intellectual certainties, well defined, packaged, and arranged for man's acceptance or rejection? How can an art, let alone such a mysterious and nonfactual art as music, have truth as its most basic meaning? We think of something as "true" if it is real; that is, it is true if there is a direct realism involved. Thus the flagpole in the schoolyard is truly a flagpole; and it is true that the sound of Johnny's practicing the piano is music. Something is also true if it corresponds to reality. The proposition that the Boston Symphony Orchestra played Haydn's "Symphony No. 88 in G Major" last evening is true only if they actually played it. Further, truth is found whenever there is a coherence established between a proposition and its parent body; that is, the proposition is necessary to more fully and systematically complete and understand the whole. Therefore, a common practice period analysis of John Dyke's "Nicaea," is truly richer than an attempt at a Franconian analysis because the former harmonizes the musical facts of the hymn in a more logical and rational manner. Finally, there is the pragmatic theory which holds that truth is known as it brings satisfaction or as it is useful. Because muzak helps cows give more milk, it is in its usefulness seen as passing the test for being true. Yet none of these is really helpful in understanding the meaning of music as truth. They might help us to verify that there is such a thing as music, or that it took place, or that a certain method of analysis explains it better than others, or that a particular music gives satisfactory results. But as for knowing music as truth, we are unenlightened.

Kierkegaard has suggested what is implicit in the Hebrew-Christian world view; that is, it is more important to be truth than to know truth. The Greeks held that truth could be found primarily in ideas, the abstract intellectualization of other-worldly concepts; but the Hebrews saw truth as a dynamic property which changes orientation toward the God of the universe, the God of all truth, the God of wonder, order, mystery, *ad infinitum*. Truth is good action: doing, vigorously applied. When Jesus said, "I am the truth," not many understood. In answer to Pilate's question about His being King, Jesus answered that He came to bear witness to the truth and that men who are of the truth, listen to Him. Pilate's rejoinder: "What is truth?" He didn't understand either. Jesus notes that men may participate in truth as they are "of the truth" or belong "to the truth;" that is, truth is a quality of being, a derivative quality coming from a right relationship, in this case, to the Truth. In a similar vein, art can be true as it manifests right internal relationships assigned it by the creator-artist.

Truth in music, then, is a quality we have formerly alluded to as rightness, a sense of internal configuration that brings the work to a logical and artistic fruition, the convincing working out of a beginning premise, a process of argumentation that brings one to the inevitable conclusion. The truth here is not a moral truth, but truth as it adheres to a God-appointed natural design at the root of material existence—a design that the artist intuitively and intellectually must subscribe to if what he creates is to be true, but also a design that can be overlooked, shortchanged, or bypassed intentionally (corruptibility) or non-intentionally (incompetence). It is the composer who establishes the truth of the musical work by his compositional action. There is no idle abstraction here. He is a dynamic mover of artistic essences.

For our scientifically-oriented culture, the question remains as to what the exact ingredients are that make a work true and in what proportion they are meted out. Unfortunately (or fortunately) there is no formula which, if followed as one follows a recipe, guarantees truth in art. We may only hint at it, for in an art such as music, which by nature is the most mysterious of all the arts, preciseness if indeed possible (which it is not) would take away its locus of being, hence dissolving all music into conventional patterns. There are principles, however, that can guide the composer, performer, and listener in the quest for establishing and apprehending truth in music, principles that when put together may very well not explain the greatness (hence the mystery) of music, so much as describe its wholesome, artistic, and right orientation. Music that is true is governed by these universal artistic principles.

Good musical conversation is contained in a time framework that marks out the perimeters or boundaries of the work. Within this stream of consciousness are musical sound events that define and give meaning to the framework. The sounds are not allowed to drift at will but are endowed with a specific time orientation related to the pulse or time ordering of the work. The principle here is that music needs to exhibit a flow, an overall feel for continuity, that moves progressively and irresistibly from beginning to end. It is not intended to hammer and drive a musical pulse into the mind—as a matter of fact the opposite is true, for rhythm means "flow," and a mind boggling "beat" may very well give the impression of immobility. The incessant flowing of the forward movement found in artistic works is related to mankind's life processes and the universal movement of time. Music mirrors and heightens time reality and in this correspondence we see the music as being true. Establishing the long line, the total sweep, the gentle but irresistible pull of temporal universality, is a challenge to the best composer. Music must move.

Part of the continuity of great music (which we have described as flow) is determined by the cohesion of the work. Isolated unrelated events are musically irrelevant. There must be an overall background unity that correlates all parts into a meaningful whole; that is to say, a unity must exist at all times, a constant, if you will, which becomes the ground of the work and from which everything springs. Unity is therefore not something that is established and then discarded in order that it might be picked up later. Unity is an organic pull, a felt quality that permeates a composition so thoroughly that every part, no matter how small, is related. There is a wholeness demonstrated here which is more than the sum of its parts—just as a man is more than arms, legs, mind and soul, and the church is more than the sum of its total members. Such unity is rooted in God. He is both one and three parts, Father, Son, and Spirit, and that which He has made exhibits a similar wholeness in that every single cell of a man, for example, carries the entire man within it. In musical terms, this similitude is called *organic unity* and is a mark of all great art. It is one of the universal principles of existence. All music, if it is to be considered art, must show it. Coherence is a mark of truth.

Within this unity every composition must also exhibit diversions at various levels. Such excursions are necessary if the music is to have movement. Nothing in the physical world is propelled forward unless there is opposition at work somewhere. A rocket channels explosive gases in the opposite direction of the intended flight path. In walking, one moves counter to the direction of the force applied against the floor by the leg and foot. (If the foot finds no traction and continues in the direction of the push we slip and perhaps stumble and fall.) In the arts there must be a correlation with the universal principle of opposites: difference, contrast, tension, inequality, and diversity. It is fact that no snowflake is exactly like another snowflake, that no two trees are precisely the same, and that people are not carbon copies of an ideal man. God made the universe with such imagination that it is one world, a living, dynamic, forward-moving creation without anything in it being exactly the same; there is contrast and there is variety. Without diversity there would only be sameness, a quality that would be not only boring but also devastatingly static. There can be no art without the tensions of related difference, and as music attempts to operate outside the universal principles God has made—in this case the principle of variety in unity—it negates its artistic validity, becoming something grotesque in its nothingness.

There is also in the musical craft of composition the necessity of subscribing to the principle of dominance. Some musical elements in the time frame are more important than others. A certain hierarchy of values is adopted by the composer in which more important features are set against the less important. Though each has a particular part to play and therefore is important to the whole, the composer knows that not everything in the work is equal. Still, he is responsible for each component's doing its part well and contributing to the overall musical statement. A like principle is at work in the created order, for God has set man over the world and God is over both. We see this principle at work in government, church, and family life. Not everyone can be a chief! Music shows universal truth as it adheres to this principle of dominance. Not every note, rhythm, or harmony can be in the foreground.

Interestingly enough, every component part of a composition needs to have intrinsic worth in and of itself. That is to say, it cannot be so dependent on its place in the composition for its worth that it has no value of its own. Such totally derived significance would insure that the less important elements in their supportive roles would tend to be weak, uninteresting, and, in effect, dull. But God has given to every man a singular standing before Him—a standing in which he is seen as unique, endowed with self-worth, and so important that He gave His Son for this one life as well as for the whole world. Though he may be one of countless millions, God cares for him as shown by His care of the sparrow and the numbering of the hairs on his head. The uniqueness that is stamped on everything in the universe is an individuality given by a caring and personal God. The artist who shows loving individual concern for the worth of even the minutiae is mirroring the way God looks at what He has made. The music demonstrates truth as each part of the composition has self-worth.

We could go on in our brief description of how music manifests truth, speaking of order and freedom, tension and release, climax, balance, symmetry, economy, and other matters related to the process of creating music. The thing to note in all of this is that art in general and music in particular evidence a relationship to the universe as they participate in the universal principles found in all of existence. Art in a sense is a reflective microcosm of the ordering of the world. As these true and unchanging principles that govern life are applied to art, or as art takes upon itself these governances, it shows a rightness or truthfulness that make it worthy and that strikes an unconscious chord of response within us. Not all art manages to reach such a high level of attainment. Moreover, much so-called music violates these principles purposely for selfish effect. The church musician in the pastoral ministry of music needs the analytical ability and intuitive feel to assign levels of value to the music he associates himself with, thereby accurately judging just how truthful a particular piece might be.

Music, then, in exhibiting artistic grace or right internal relationships, shows truth and, in being true, is part of the revelation of God to man. Hence we cannot dismiss it lightly as being unimportant or peripheral. They who hold that man's attention should be riveted only to the Word and that everything else should be excluded have misunderstood the Scriptures. While the Bible is the final rule of faith and practice and puts knowledge into a proper framework, it never should be thought of as the sum total of all man is to know of God. God has made man that man might discover, and in the discovery learn more of truth in general. In the *Imago Dei,* He has equipped man wonderfully well for fulfilling the creative and cultural mandates, mandates which in their fulfilling reveal more of the truth of God which is to be found everywhere in all disciplines. In its own right, music tells us more of the Almighty Creator—revelation which comes only through the medium of music. Calvin Seerveld quotes Abraham Kuyper as saying,

Art is no fringe that is attached to the garment, and no amusement that is added to life, but a most serious power in our present existence. Art reveals ordinances of creation which neither science, nor politics, nor religious life, nor even Biblical revelation can bring to light.[7]

Music has a task which goes far beyond the average church musician's wildest imagination. Music as a revelation of eternal mysteries opens a vast frontier for new development.

III. Beyond the Explicitness of Words

Truth in the Biblical record is not always crystal clear. Note the many Bible translations and versions, each of which attempts some further clarification of the "real" meaning, the thousands of books written to explain and interpret, and the great men of faith who disagree as to the significance of a particular text. It is a book shrouded in mystery simply because (1) the subject matter, the infinite, is so far removed from the finite; and (2) the confines of language make communication of the numinous difficult. The Word of God ultimately lies beyond the word-symbols. The revelation of God coming through words is without a doubt, as we have already said, the most exact medium for the transfer of information. But even in Scripture itself, stated facts are sometimes left far behind and the writer breaks into poetry, story, parable, or song. Preciseness is not necessarily a guarantee that the true reality behind the words will be made known. It is here that music can help. Often the Scripture attempts to utter the unutterable, to speak the unspeakable, to make known vast mysteries that are beyond the scope of word intelligibility. Music can help open to us these and other unutterable, unspeakable mysteries: (1) by virtue of the musical art's being inherently mysterious in its abstractness and truthful quality; (2) by its being able to explore life-truths in general; and (3) by its exploring musically the truth of a given subject matter.

First, music's natural ambiguity and abstractness, plus its being truth in the sense of having been inspired and created with that sense of rightness that comes by adherence to God's universal world-life artistic principles, gives it a quality of mystery. The mystery of the work remains, no matter how much analysis and explanation takes place in the search for musical value, because art has a life of its own, and, like the spark of human life, does not easily give up its secrets. The dissections, ponderings, and investigations a musical composition might be subjected to reveal much about it and are helpful to us, but when it comes right down to saying what it is that makes it artistically alive and vital, we must confess that we do not know. And this is the wonder of music's mystery. We know so much about it—performing, listening, and creating—but still that inspiration, that vision, that creative spark of genius can only be expressed in terms of music and known in terms of mystery. Music should become prized for this mysterious quality in our musical ministry, for where the Biblical record needs a feeling tone, a sense of mystery, an aliveness which the words by themselves do not have, God has provided us with music.

Second, music explores the mysteries of the essences of life: tension and release, struggle and conquest, movement and stillness, sound and silence, growth and decline, affirmation and rejection, life and death, and so on.[8] They are dealt with symbolically rather than factually. The musical symbol refers to that which is vague. It is known when thought about, but is normally seen through a haze, or, depending on our life experience, is unknown. These essences affect man in everyday life but are hidden from him, for they are truths to be known and felt in the unguarded moments of living. The composer takes these essences, these truths of life, puts them into another context, and returns them to man for his edification. One finds in music a great ability to deal with these hidden mysteries. For one thing, the processes of musical composition are, as we have seen, life processes. One only needs to hear the music to note its struggles, its conquests, its still moments, the tensions, the climaxes, its unity and diversity. Life is there. Sound in motion is life in motion. It somehow stirs man to his depths and he is moved, transported to the heavenly realm, and given a new vision of life. For another thing, music is superbly equipped to handle these essences because they are more truths than they are facts, and in music's being true there is a natural proclivity for revealing that truth, mysterious though it may be.

A distinction needs to be made here between fact and truth. Facts are only road signs that point to truth. They may be true in themselves, but they are not truth as we are using the term, for truth can never be completely captured by anything in creaturely existence. We can know more of the truth of something but never everything about it, for that would make one omniscient, an attribute of God only. The saying that "Christ died for our sins," or noting the historical fact of the crucifixion is not the truth of the redemptive act—it only points to it. The fact of an antique chair is not the truth of the chair. Peter's walking on and subsequent falling into the water are facts that only point to the truth of the matter. More needs to be discovered. The facts need to be probed for meanings because truth is a deeper, fuller, more complete reality than that which is produced by facts. In our life explorations of the Word, relationships, self, education, experience, or what have you, we come to know more of the truth. Facts just confront us with the more basic questions of ethical, moral, theological, physical, artistic, and psychological significance and require interpretation, correlation, exploration, and application.

> But what is truth? Is truth fact? Or, in a theological frame of reference, is truth doctrine? Certainly truth includes fact and doctrine, but truth is not limited to them. The archaeologist finds the fragments of a vase, but his interest in the vase goes far beyond the fact of the vase in his hands, and the characteristics which he, as well as the merest amateur, can readily observe. To say, "This is a red clay vase" does not tell the truth about it, and he wants to know the truth as fully as he can. And so he asks many more questions: When was it made? Where was it made? Who made it? Where did he get his materials? Does it show that its fashioner loved or hated his work? How was it used? Does its resting place show that it was prized or discarded, broken, in a junk-heap? What does

this vase reveal about the life of the people who produced and used it? We could go on, and the archaeologist does. The point is, however, that the fact of the vase is not the truth of the vase.[9]

Perhaps facts might be said to be certainties which, though correct, are by themselves sterile and cold but nevertheless have the capacity of intimating deeper realities which lead to a fuller knowledge of life. Obviously some facts are dead ends. "Red is not green" is a true fact, but that is the end of it. However, it is possible to use red and green in a painting which captures the painter's point of view in such a manner that some of the truth which he sees inherent in the subject is communicated to the viewer. Of course the truth of a man, the meaning of his life, could never be completely shown through the visual art, but the artist attempts, by exploring the fact of his face and then emphasizing, distorting, and featuring certain elements to il-luminate a little more of the truth of the man. And we are edified in ap-prehending his work.

Carl Halter maintains that music explores the vast area between fact and truth, the territory between complete and full understanding of life-truths (which we have termed struggle and conquest, tension and release, affirma-tion and rejection, and so on) and the fact of the musical symbol. In our participation as listeners in the seeking out of mysterious meanings in this immense space between the fact of life as embodied in musical symbols and the fuller truth of life we become changed, never again to be really the same because our understanding of life has broadened and deepened—not that we can verbalize our deepened vision. The experience of really seeing, feel-ing, knowing, and interpreting a sunrise from the top of a coastal mountain, for example, can never be adequately explained to someone else. The facts may be presented to them (e.g., "I saw a glorious sunrise of pink tinged with . . . "), but this does not communicate the truth of the matter—truth that deepens one's perspective on God's creation. The visual experience operates between the fact of the sunrise and the full truth of God in crea-tion, and words can never fully communicate the experience. So it is with the musical investigation of life-essences. We just cannot adequately speak in words about what is first a musical event. We can analyze and discuss the parts of the work which show mounting tension and those that bring release, for example, but the depth of the struggle cannot be known outside the ex-perience of participatory listening. The music itself investigates life-essences and processes and brings us to an enlarged vision of the deeper reality of these truths. Music must be heard and known as something more than mere pleas-ant sounds for our amusement. It must be seen as a serious attempt to know more of the truth of our world—truth which is ultimately God's.

In dealing with the categories of mystery, awe, love, acceptance, rejection, or what have you, we find categories that music explores in terms of its own theological discipline of ordered sound. These are not linked with any par-ticular explicit God orientation but are akin to an implicit musical version of general revelation. These mysterious truths of which we speak are unut-terable, untranslatable, wordless, and unique. It is though we have some perplexing matter suddenly revealed and we exclaim in wonder, "Of course!"

only to perceive by hindsight that we never realized that there was a perplexing problem in the first place. Music, as it explores "the elements of truth which are above, beneath, around, behind, and beyond the fact,"[10] gives us a little more of the truth of God, His creation and what it means to be a man in a world that is fallen but which through God's grace can be redeemed.

Up to this point we have discussed how music can explore and reveal truths that are beyond the scope of word intelligibility because of its mysteriousness and since it probes for life-meanings. Now we come to an area which has much applied value for the church musician, that of music's ability to discover the hidden meaning of a word idea or text. The Scripture, in being confined to word symbols, often needs the intuitive help of music to express more fully the deeper reality of the word symbol. We have noted that a "dry" recital of facts is often incapable of expressing the fuller truth of the fact. Particularly here, being concerned with the numinous category in which matters of divine mystery should cause man to tremble in awe before the Almighty if he could only get a glimpse of the truth, we are attempting to discover music's potential for helping us more fully know the divine hinted at in the text of a song.

Technically, it is not the words that are the most important element of a vocal solo or a choral piece. As Susanne Langer has put it, "Every work [of art] has its being in only one order of art;" music "ordinarily swallows words and action creating (thereby) opera, oratorio, or song."[11] What we find in the highest choral art is that the word idea communicates to the listener specific facts for which the musical symbol stands. We have then a very good idea of the beginning orientation of the composer and can more specifically follow his musical working out or exploration of the truth hinted at by the fact. Knowing the words to "Ode to Joy," for example, gives us a more definite frame of reference in which to understand what Beethoven is saying in the last movement of *Symphony 9*. The pathos we feel in the "Crucifixus" of the J.S. Bach *B Minor Mass* is directed toward Christ's crucifixion because we know the words. The words, then, direct us to the specific facts, but the music itself, in its own way, goes beyond the fact. "Joyful, joyful, we adore Thee," and "He was crucified, dead and buried," as statements, do not engender the mystery of godly ecstacy or despair; it takes the music to lead us toward the feeling and knowing of the truth of these facts. We can never really know how it does this—it remains a mystery. We can only give thanks that it does.

IV. Imparting a Sense of Mystery

Both Archibald Davison and Austin Lovelace feel that one of the commonalities between music and religion is mystery. Lovelace says:

The mind of man cannot comprehend the wonder of God; it can only see the occasional flashes of light which shine through the glory holes of life. In the awesome areas of life's mystery, music helps man to express the inexpressible.[12]

However, this is not to suggest that the mystery which is part of the truth of God is known and felt automatically by the worshipper, though at its highest and best, worship should have an overwhelming sense of the *mysterium tremendum.* As a matter of fact, the Christian, even though filled with gratitude, penitence, aspiration, and communion, will have to cultivate that sense of wonder that accompanies the worship of the Almighty. Printing a reminder in the Sunday bulletin or announcing from the pulpit that "The Lord is in His holy temple: let all the earth keep silence before Him" will not do the trick. For man to have full realization of the mystery and awe inherent in the worship of Almighty God, the truth of God's transcendence must be known and felt from the inside out and the outside in. One takes his "shoes" off—he is on holy ground.

Perhaps remedial measures need to be taken to restore mystery, awe, and wonder to their rightful place as context qualities for worship. Surely music cannot do it by itself, but what can be done is to insure that the music which is used helps foster these important characteristics. For example, music of the popular type that is made for reassurance, for immediate comprehensibility, for cozy comfortableness, rather than for prophetic utterance, takes away any sense of the unknown or of mystery. Its whole thrust is toward that which is known as simply, as immediately, and as easily as possible. There is no mystery, no awe, for everything is understandable down to the stereotyped formulas. To call forth awe in a worshipper. however, which Walter Nathan suggests is the ground of faith, a work of art must make demands on the hearer. It must establish that ambiguity in music is not something to be afraid of but to be embraced. It is not merely literal strangeness or otherworldly association which endows music with transcendental value, but its artistic value, its true-ness. No matter how familiar one becomes with the Bach *St. Matthew Passion,* it never loses its sense of awe and wonder. Music of worth, though it may not be in the same category as Bach's passions, is the music that best helps foster mystery in worship. Herman Berlinski says:

> Why is it necessary to define the basic laws of art music in connection with the topic of this article? The definition of these basic laws [principles of time, tendency gratification, form] became necessary because these laws of art music are the laws which impart to music its transcendental value.[13]

Artistic merit must be the primary consideration in finding music with a numinous category of value, and unfamiliarity a secondary consideration.

V. Summary

The minister of music, as a theological interpreter of the Word in terms of music, finds himself face to face with the element of God's transcendence. God is holy and man trembles in His presence. He is "wholly other" and man stands in awe of Him, for God is the eternal mystery. Such concepts presented as facts point the Christian in the direction of the deeper reality of God. However, music, in being "true" by mirroring universal artistic principles, by being new and freshly creative, also explores and celebrates, reveals, probes and illuminates more fully the numinous, and more specific theological frames of reference in the context of worship as it translates them into deeply known and felt qualities. A music program must incorporate music that can deal effectively with such categories. Music that is artistically stale, that does not cause the listener to utilize his intelligence and imagination, that takes an easy and (overly) familiar way, that creates the mood of perfect ease and contentment, is music that has lost its capacity to engender a sense of awe and wonder. It is music that has lost its emotive power and its transcendental appeal. Anthems and hymns that are mildly sweet and pretty, emphasizing trite sentimentality, are effective destroyers of awe. The director of music should avoid such expressions. Music may be interesting, relevant to life, personal, knowable, and even dramatic, but music must be artistically worthy, for with artistic grace as a foundation stone, music will be able to capture and present the truth of the transcendent God. Music will be a gateway into that realm in which the worshipper will more fully grasp the truth of God's mystery and more fully experience that sense of awe that comes from a fuller realization of His Holiness. The veiled strains of the *mysterium tremendum* are in the notes.

9

CONCLUSION

I. The Crucifixion

The crucifixion and resurrection are the focal points of Christianity, events so stunning that they have become the crossroads of history. Even as the Old Testament is centered around a single event—the Exodus—so the New Testament sees the death and resurrection of our Lord in a similar manner. The crucifixion and resurrection are the two main events in God's disclosure of Himself to mankind. Without them all other knowledge of God cannot be seen in its correct perspective.

The crucifixion and the rising of Christ from the dead are really a single event. One without the other invalidates both. Paul declares that "Christ died for our sins according to the Scriptures" (I Corinthians 15:3) but he also says that "if Christ be not raised, your faith is in vain; ye are yet in your sins" (I Corinthians 15:17). Only together can they be said to complete the redemptive initiative taken by God, though, as in any other larger truth, breaking it down into smaller units aids in our understanding and edification. Thus we shall look to the crucifixion and resurrection separately for whatever they have to say to the musician, and then, seeing the event as a totality, we will attempt to find an approach to the pastoral ministry of music.

The crucifixion marks the completion of the incarnation, Jesus being born as a man and dying as a man. Though initially He lowered Himself in His coming to earth as a babe in the flesh, in being crucified He ultimately "sank into greater depths than any other human being had ever done; He fell into that abyss into which we deserve to fall . . . no one as a dying man anticipated Hell as He did."[1] We see in this final humiliation of Jesus the absolute love God has for man, a love He showed to us by deed, a love on which every minister of music should model his own feeling for those who are entrusted to his pastoral care. The humility demonstrated in the Christmas story is a far cry from the humility He endured in the cruelty, shame, and injustice of the cross. Likewise the musician is called to suffer as Christ suffered, to know that love which gives up everything *in toto*. It is this quiet, gentle, meek, patient, long-suffering, and nonsensational example of our Lord that will carry the church musician through his own hours of despair, self-abjuration, and absence of that which he believes is due him.

Jesus' death was the supreme sacrifice in which He bore fully the condemnation of man. His propitiatory work shows His love to us in that He freely chose to die to atone for man's sin. His suffering was like no other suffering; His agony was a spiritual as well as a physical one. The travail in giving man new life was a travail that was redemptive, a travail instructive for all those who would affirm the Christ-life, a travail which in some mysterious way shows that for man, or God in man's context, suffering and discipline are part of his humanity, part of his condition, and part of that which serves goodness.

The artistic world is not exempt from the need for this renunciation discipline. It is the necessary path that leads to bringing forth the new. Struggle surfaces in the art work, but it can only be fully known by the creator himself. As in human birth, travail is a prelude to the consummation of the work, the particular art object in question being, as it were, begotten rather than just "made." This is not to say that all artistic endeavor has come by way of the cross—far from it. But that which breaks new ground imaginatively and with integrity comes from the hand of the master who has dealt with the discipline of his craft, who wrestles and struggles to bring to light his vision of some shred of reality, and who does so in travail. The performer, too, does not merely wile away his time amusing himself as he practices and studies his scores. He participates in personal renunciation of lesser things for the necessary discipline to become a great technician and interpreter of the world's great composers. And the listener will never come to know what music is all about if he does not sit at its feet to learn (which often means frustration, a cloudy understanding which is gradually lifted as one struggles to master the unknown) and exhibit a priority which often sets aside the more "pleasurable."

Church music, of all music, must be influenced by the cross if it is to be Biblically based. Composers, performers, and congregations alike must not seek to exempt the death of our Lord from the impact it will have on their music, for the cross shows that the self-seeking pleasure syndrome inherent in the comfortable banalities of much church music is a lie. Both Amos Wilder and Eric Routley speak frankly about the church and its normal artistic and theological posture:

> It must be taken as a working premise that . . . no good art will be facile or easy-come-by, or borrowed or second hand. A really significant piece of art—and how much more for the church—will cost not only tuition in craft but austere spiritual discipline.[2]

> There is a danger that in the composition and practice of church music the church will always turn to what is easy and familiar, seeking to bring men to Christ by a route which by-passes the way of the cross.[3]

The cross speaks to the church musician of the need for what we have called renunciation discipline, the setting aside of one's ease for the sake of paying the full price. Much Victorian church music, the American gospel song, and the pop which began to come into the church in the late fifties are examples of music, which, musically speaking, omit the cross. In general, they lack the musical "bite" to express anything but sentimentalized and romanticized notions of Christianity; there is no struggle here, no musical wrestling, no humble strength. The whole impression is one of comfortableness and niceness. While it is necessary to be understanding of the composing, dissemination, and usage of such music without being harshly judgmental in attitude, it must be said that it has had and is having a large part to play in promoting Christian infantilism in which being a Christian means a life of plenty, freedom from suffering, the use of God as a personal valet to meet one's self-wants, a certain status or acceptability, and a comfortable niche in the world—in short, to have a God whose purpose is to serve man. Much of this music, in being trite, repetitious, dull, and musically silly (even nauseous), gives off the general aura of the comfortableness of the rocking chair, not the discipline of the cross. We need to see that the cross and one's being crucified daily with Christ as Paul says, musically requires that which does more than console, lull to sleep, or appear pretty, nice, and entertaining. It requires a music which in its musical integrity will be heard as disciplined, vigorous, even stark, requiring the listener to "lean forward" in the pew to catch its meaning rather than sit back and be "muzaked." This music will require suffering and travail in its own right as it confronts the worshipper. That it does so is to know musically a little more of the reality of the cross.

II. The Resurrection

The resurrection as the culmination of the crucifixion is so important to the Christian religion that Emil Brunner writes:

> Without the resurrection, all discussion of the mystery of the person and saving work of Jesus Christ—indeed, all claims of the Christian faith—would be without meaning. But they have meaning because He is risen.[4]

If Jesus had remained in the grave, He could not have been the Messiah, for a dead Christ is no Christ at all. He could not have been who He said He was without being the victor over sin and death. The entire New Testament is conceived around the resurrection either in mentioning Christ's rising specifically or by being written with the understanding of its being an accomplished fact. Our earliest recorded sermons by the apostles give much attention to Christ's rising, and they became models for the preaching of the early church. The resurrection rallied the demoralized disciples, gave them new hope, and became the foundation of the New Testament church, having a much more prominent place in their witness than in ours today. The first day of the week was the celebration of the miracle of Christ's breaking death's bonds; thus every Sunday became an Easter celebration! They knew there could be no Christianity without the centrality of the resurrection of our Lord. It is an essential doctrine needing a new emphasis in our time not only for preaching but also for the church's music.

We see here a miracle with a depth of meaning that goes beyond the finite mind. It is the resurrection that opens to man new life, a promise for the future. It is that which breaks the bonds of the now and shows us what can be. In the resurrection we have the completion of our redemption, and in our redemption we have a whole new orientation beyond the temporal (although at the present we are still confined to the temporal). But we have a vision which gives us new imaginative insights into what is not, what could be, and what someday will be. In more direct terms, it is the resurrection that frees man's spirit, sets him to dreaming, and activates his imagination. Even as the cross was instructive for disciplined craftsmanship, so the resurrection is instructive for creative originality. The redeemed have opened to them a life of newness, freshness, exaltation, and creativity which should affect their entire living, including their art.

Music, which is not bound by the literally seen, tasted, smelled, or touched material of our world, is in an enviable place as far as creativity is concerned. The resurrection speaks to us of the eternal, of immortality, of timelessness, and of boundlessness. Music deals with these qualites somewhat more naturally than the other arts, for it is concerned with the ethereal, the beyond, the "music of the spheres." It is not discovery like astronomy, physics, or biology; it is an investigation of that which in a sense is beyond our world yet in our world—an incarnation of sound shaped into something that attempts to transcend the world. Man has always been restless with the beautiful, perhaps even seeing in it a faint image of the true freedom and perfection which the Christian knows to be in Christ the risen Lord. It is the resurrection that completes redemption and opens up new vistas of intuition, of creativity, of imagination, of originality, and creative energy for every man.

It would seem, then, at first glance that we have come full circle, for we began with the doctrine of creation and its implications for creativity and now once again we are back face to face with it. However, it is not that we have come full circle so much as we have followed a continuum of development in which we have now a new creation, and Christ—the second Adam—is the first fruit of that new creation. In seeing art through the eyes of full redemption and resurrection, we must agree with Brunner, who feels that in one sense art "has more to do with Redemption than with Creation."[5] Especially is it true of music, which can bring us closer to the nebulous, but real, feelings of the need for completion, to the breaking point with our world, to the casting aside of the restraints of the flesh as was done in the resurrection. Music can never do this itself, of course, but it can point to man's need for breaking free from the temporal. Whereas our study of the doctrine of creation is concerned more with the activity of this world, the resurrection is concerned more with the next. The resurrection opens to man the possibility of having his present artistic works inspired by worlds unknown—an intuitive, imaginative plane influenced by the perfection of a new heaven and a new earth.

There is a certain level of artistic living available to those of us who see the creative gift through the resurrection if we will only appropriate it. We find in Christ's rising both the wellspring for creativity and a call to creativity. That is to say, in Christ, creative living is ours, and Christ will give us new vision, new originality, and new artistic grace. But we must feel the need to heed His call to new life (even in art), see the urgency for doing so, and know that living below the intent of the resurrected life is unnecessary poverty. It is not simply that imaging God in terms of musical privation is bad, as we noted in the section on the *Imago Dei*. There is a more sterling need to fully appropriate the bounty of God's creative riches; that is, in the resurrection we come as close as we can to materializing life eternal. Yet we have life eternal now even in our fleshly state. Therefore, as Christians we have every reason to live as close as we can to the heavenly realm—even in music. To do less is to cast away, musically speaking, the resurrection. Why live on crackers and cheese when Christ has spread before us a sumptuous banquet? Life in the resurrection of our Lord, a life in the Spirit of God himself, is an unfathomable life of creative imagination—words fail us and we need to turn to music!

The crucifixion and resurrection together open up to the Christian and to the church a whole new way of looking at life. Redemption means that the arts, in dealing with the beautiful, will have a new and special meaning for the Christian. Life in the Spirit, redeemed life, has no business with the petty, the trivial, the mediocre, but rather with richness and fullness, life pregnant with the promise of God, who is concerned with the right, the true, the just, and the pure. Of course there will be flexibility to include the state of all men, for we are not attempting to find a certain music for the church in the narrow sense. Within the personal and churchly cultural context of our people we seek music that will strive toward the perfection of the resurrection. Because we have new life, we as Christians are in the best position to realize what redemption means or should mean for the arts in general and music in particular. The church music program, because it is made up of Christians, can and should be a highly polished mirror that collects and shines forth redemption creativity, a creativity of the cross and a creativity of the resurrection, a creativity of renunciatory discipline, and a creativity of boundless imagination.

A church music program, as part of the activity of the redeemed, must clearly reflect a Biblical world-view. Ideally speaking, the church is a place where God's full intentions for man can be realized. The redemption restores to man his original place before God, and while not yet perfect, man has new channels from God through which redeemed creativity can flow. The artistic dimension of life, often estranged from the church because of many people's unwitting determination to see authenticity in the musical expression of praise and witness as unessential, is as much a recipient of God's grace as are other areas of life. As a regenerated man, the Christian sees all of life as God's and he knows that the arts

> belong within the community of faith because they belong to man as God's creature, because they are part of the wholeness of the life He has given us, and because in and through them we may enrich our creaturely life and praise Him who is our God and King.[6]

The church music program, as a microcosm of Biblical creative intentions, is the place where every member can discover, improve, and utilize his musical gift. But it is only as one understands and appreciates the theological dimensions of his musical action that the true significance of that action, of that gift, comes into focus. Regenerate man sings and sings well because he of all people has something to sing about. The God of the universe came, died, and rose for him, and that is worth more than he ever will be able to express. But he can give the full worth, as he knows it, back to God. He ascribes a worth-ship or worship to his Lord, a worship with the first fruits of his labor, a worship that is costly, a worship that stems from pure *agape* love. The musician who has a right heart cannot do less.

No matter how much we would like to assume that church music is just entertainment, just pure neutral agent without value, or just aesthetic gratification, the crucifixion and resurrection show us otherwise. As part of *new* life, church music, in its composition, performance, and appreciation, must come by way of the cross, the way of suffering, and the way of discipline. Then the resurrection will be shown forth in joy, exuberance, and exultation. This music of the redeemed will be like no music on earth. It will be a music founded in the Word, a music firmly planted in the realites of this world, and reaped transformed by the boundless imagination and creativity of heaven.

III. A Contrapuntal Dynamic

The crucifixion and resurrection suggest a way to make usable sense out of the varying theological ideas presented in the preceding pages, for here we see a fundamental principle common to mankind's existence: life leads to death and death to life. A kernel of wheat falls into the ground and dies, and a new stalk arises. The essence of man's life lies in the cycle and tension of natural opposites: summer and winter, seedtime and harvest, night and day, movement and countermovement, negative and positive, victory and defeat, and so on. In the theological realm, Christ lives because of the cross; man lives because he has died and been reborn; the first shall be last and the last shall be first; it is only in losing one's life that he truly finds it; we are justified yet sinners; it is in giving that one receives; in weakness we are strong, and on and on. The result of the death and rising of our Lord was, as foreordained by God, the redemption of mankind. But redemption as the answer to man's sinful dilemma came through the balanced process of two extremes—in this case the life and death of Jesus, the greatest paradox of all. To experience the new life, man's old nature must die. That is to say, there is always the crucifixion to go through to get to the resurrection. There is first the agony and then the ecstacy. Man's dilemma is quite different from Christ's atoning work, of course. Being man, he is caught up between humbleness and exaltedness, imperfection and perfection. Christ's work has made him perfect in God's eyes as far as his sin goes, but the fullness of his salvation is something he must discover and rediscover as the Lord teaches, leads, and guides him through pain leading to joy over and over again for the rest of his life. The full meaning of redemption can never be fully known now. But we can and indeed must press on toward the mark of the high calling we have been given.

Full redemptive life, then, comes through the paradox of pain and joy, yes and no, freedom and discipline; musically put, a counterpoint. Church music as part of redeemed life is governed by a similiar process, which is to say that church music must proceed contrapuntally.

The word counterpoint comes from the Latin *punctus contra punctum*, point counter point, or musically, "note against note," "melody against melody." It is used to describe music in which independent melodic lines (themes) are combined so as to affirm their collective dependence on one another.

A dialogue is set up between these horizontal (melodic) lines and the resulting vertical (harmonic) chords, thus shaping the particular design of the musical fabric (texture). The chordal structure, coming from the combining of the melodies, cannot be so derivative that it makes no musical sense; nor can the "independent" melodies themselves become totally "dependent" because they are governed (to a greater or lesser degree) by harmonic considerations. This process of directional balance is a type of musical argument in which "note against note" produces "conversation" between the horizontal and vertical aspects of music, and between the individual melodic lines. In such a contrapuntal "conversation" the texture shows a balance weighted in favor of the linear or horizontal emphasis—a directional balance that allows each individual line (soprano, alto, tenor, bass, and so on) its melodic independence first, and only secondarily harmonizes the line so as to produce a satisfactory succession of chords. As Walter Piston puts it, counterpoint is the "interplay of musical agreement and disagreement."[7]

In making his ever-present, unavoidable musical decisions and judgments, the church musician must learn to weigh the relative merits of one action against the other in the light of theological propositions and counterpropositions within a given situation. Practically speaking, this means that, instead of striving for a certain music, he is striving for a faith commitment of people. That which he does musically should come about because of what he knows about God and what God has to say concerning people in their various context conditions. We must remember the gospel admonition to balance concern for the poor with costly acts of devotion to God. A church musician's stance cannot be a hard and fast one. There will be movement and countermovement. It will be dynamic, which is to say that the music done in any given situation will reflect the counterpoint of the various and often opposite truths we have put forth.

This is a far cry from the music director's doing what the people want or arbitrarily using only "great" music, or what is even worse, having a loose-ended variety in the music program in order to please every taste—something for everyone. The balance we are after is a prophetic one, a contrapuntal balance that edges people closer and closer to where they need to be in order to participate more completely in the full scope of the redeemed life. It is a balance that is directional, pointing the congregation toward a more closely aligned musical understanding with the Word, a pull toward even greater and deeper musical and theological truth.

The pastoral ministry of music is not static. It is a life pilgrimage toward a musical-spiritual maturity, a maturity that reflects God's Word in musical action—action that proceeds from the themes that have appeared many times in our investigation. Note the contrapuntal tension in the following points which serve as a foundation to a workable philosophy of church music:

1. Church music, made and used by redeemed man, must be creative. No church music should be trite, banal, hackneyed, or stereotyped. Man is less

than he should be when his music is less than it should be. All church music must exhibit the breaking of new ground imaginatively and with integrity. If it is uncreative and does not show forth musical worth, it does not belong in church.

2. The objective analysis of the worth of music is only important as it indicates that the best that can be done is being done and that growth is taking place. Church music must correspond to people's abilities, cultural environment, and insight. Strivings of people come before objective musical worth.

3. Mankind, made in the image of a Creator, has a nature, capabilities, and peculiar gifts which firmly and unequivocably give him a place of honor, dignity, sovereignty, and exaltedness in the world.

4. Our basic posture is one of dependence, humility and service; our leadership is modeled after the scriptural example of the servant image culminating in Jesus.

5. The Christian faith seeks a church music that exhibits a balance between reason and emotion. Music must have good craftsmanship and exhibit a warmth which comes from feeling identification with the music.

6. Church music must proceed in a manner that shows the faith action required of the Christian life. True artistic adventure in music should be seen as a musical expression of the fact that we are pilgrims walking by faith.

7. Church music should be incarnational in that the medium ought to be correlative to the gospel. Musical truth is important, for music always witnesses. It is possible to negate the gospel content through poor (untruthful) form. For example, the tenor of the gospel is not popularity at any price, for when church music seeks popularity through pop music, the musical form gives a distorted view of the full gospel.

8. The incarnation suggests that God came to man in a form to which man could relate. Relevancy is important in that there must be some common ground between parties. A congregation's musical profile must be taken into account in choosing music. It is imperative that there be a common musical frame of reference between church music and the listener.

9. God's otherness, His transcendence and mystery are best shown through music that exhibits high artistic integrity and is uniquely fresh, singulary new, or not fully known. On the other hand, immanence requires church music to have a special feeling identification with, and relevancy for, the listener.

The agreement and disagreement between these themes is the "point against point" upon which a beneficial theological counterpoint is based. For example, if a specific situation warrants it, we temper our legitimate concern for high creativity (#1 above) with the contrasting thrust of stewardship (#2 above). As the congregation develops under prophetic leadership and its musical faith-walk matures, other doctrinal topics will be judiciously added. The music will begin to reflect God's intentions for His people.

A philosophy of church music cannot be based on the theory that the purpose of a music ministry is to serve music (aesthetic approach); neither should it be based on the theory that the purpose of a music ministry is to serve people (pragmatic approach). The purpose of a coherent, comprehensive, and creative music ministry is to serve the Lord. Music becomes the full gospel in action. Then and only then will it have an authoritative prophetic word that will speak to both music and people, communicator and communicant.

The church musician must base his philosophy on the Word of God. The theological topics we have mentioned must constantly be weighed and evaluated in the light of each other in the context of the immediate situation. Musical methodology, based on theology, will not be static but dynamic, not harmonic but contrapuntal. The church musician will not be a musical objectivist; neither will he be a musical subjectivist. He will be a theological musical situationalist, meaning that he will have objective standards that are subjective in that they are situationally/theologically determined. Theological musical situationalism is the ground from which springs the pastoral ministry of music.

The goals and methods of the pastoral church music ministry will be dictated by a directional balance in the counterpoint of our theological formulations as they relate to the individual congregation. A working philosophy of church music recognizes where people are and also where they ought to be. The shape of one's musical ministry is determined by the direction in which the church needs to progress. Everything the musician does must be prophetic; that is, it must have a cutting edge that causes the congregation to discard little by little the excess baggage of poor musical-theological orientation and move toward a maturing musical expression of a maturing faith.

It is precisely this directional balance, this need to be prophetic, this moving toward a fuller musical expression and witness, that gives integrity to a ministry of music. The question is not one of present status (of what music is being sung and how well it is being done, or of having variety in one's program), but one of moving toward the mark of the ideal held up for us in Scripture. We cannot allow our congregations to become complacent, closed to anything worthwhile, because of a self-satisfied condition. Yet we cannot alienate them musically. The work of a virile ministry of music is its active push toward that which is known to be the highest and best for the right reasons. The heart will then be right before God and men.

The course charted by one's understanding of a particular congregation and by the Biblical mandate to live out life creatively will not be turned aside by a tempestuous sea. Society's blitz of changing values, ordinarily causing the director of music great uncertainty, will be overcome by the musical-theological vision of what he knows to be the will of God. His course is set by what God has revealed to us about His expectations for His chosen people. Come what may, the minister of music can rest assured that it is both needful and possible to move steadily toward our goal, even though at times one must tack against the wind.

Relying on theology rather than on aestheticism or pragmatism gives a unique perspective. We have the highest musical standards, for they come from Scripture. Knowing the ideal, we strive with our people where they are. A directional balance, contrapuntally tuned to our seemingly contradictory theological themes, a balance that moves toward the musical-spiritual goal, is the framework of a workable music ministry. It is a ministry founded in the Word.

IV. Application: A Working Counterpoint

To further clarify the process of using such a contrapuntal method, it would be well to include here an actual church application. We will first review in some detail the "contrapuntal" method, then discuss "collective congregational progress" which is so very necessary to prophetic music ministry, and finally construct a hypothetical church situation that will serve to demonstrate a working theological counterpoint.

We have described in Chapters 2 through 8 a number of theological topics that are the underpinnings of a Biblical pastoral music ministry. In this chapter we have outlined a philosophical methodology that allows for a coherent, comprehensive, and creative use of the individual viewpoints (no matter how different) of each of these doctrinal themes. We have termed such a philosophical approach "contrapuntal," for, like musical counterpoint, it is a disciplined process that allows each "voice" or "theme" its own independence and autonomy while simultaneously acknowledging the necessity of combining with the others. This theological counterpoint is the methodological design, fluid and flexible yet uncompromising in its integrity, upon which theological musical situationalism is based.

Proceeding from the paradoxical element noted in the crucifixion and resurrection of our Lord, it has seemed logical to develop for the music ministry a working counterpoint in which the "agreement" and "disagreement" of our Biblical themes could be (directionally) "harmonized." Such conversation back and forth between the topics developed in these pages is a vital nerve center of the pastoral ministry of music. It is the very heart of theological musical situationalism and is perhaps the most important single factor in the musical and spiritual success of music ministry.

As we have already mentioned, a working counterpoint will be dynamic, having a flexibility capable of accommodating every situation. We cannot meet the needs of a changing society by championing a music ministry that is guided in whole or in part by aesthetic or pragmatic legalistic attitudes, rules, and regulations. Our fast-moving world demands that our music ministry be fluid or, in musical terminology, melodic. Modern-day congregations, pastors, music directors, singers, and instrumentalists must adopt a philosophy that is able to impact culture without being absorbed and ultimately destroyed by it. A position capable of accommodating change but which is also capable of being disciplined by the changeless Word is necessary. We have termed such an orientation as contrapuntal. To the uninitiated this approach to music ministry lacks both the comfort of definitive boundaries and the intoxication of unrestrained license. At first it may seem strange and unsettling. However, the hospitable integrity found in a contrapuntal methodology based on the Word will banish any fear of newly-found freedom/discipline. It is as if we no longer are under the "law" but are continually in the process of discovering "grace." We are freed from *having* to do this or that music either because it is "good" or because it brings "results." The music we do will depend on where the congregation is in its musical "faith-walk" and on the direction it needs to go to continue in that walk.

The question is routinely raised, "How realistic is it to expect musical advancement in the life of a congregation?'' In a mobile society where there is a constant transfer of new members into the church and where the church is experiencing the addition of many new converts, is it likely that there will be any collective musical progress? Moreover, how accurately can a music director discern the collective average of a congregation's musical comprehension, or, as Routley puts it, their musical "center of gravity?"[8]

Such questions are important as well for other areas in the corporate life of the church: preaching, giving, education, missionary outreach, social concerns, evangelism. Can the "people of God" move forward as a group? Is corporate progress in the realm of possibility? For example, if the pastor has preached a series of sermons on tithing and over a period of months has led his congregation into a collective practice of the principle, will he need to spend the next year doing the exact same thing in order to teach the five percent of the congregation who are new?

No matter how we answer these questions, there remains the fact that individual congregations do have collective personalities and profiles. Attend a pastor's council and listen to the comments: such and such a church is "loving," or "has never reached its potential," or is a "musical church," or "has a real vision for missions," or "is learning the meaning of the body ministry," or "is a giving church." Upon moving to a new community, ask about possible church homes and listen to the varied descriptive comments. Congregations do have collective vision, collective personality, collective spiritual tone, and a collective musical "faith-walk."

Congregational profiles are the result of many things (people's individual background, tastes, educational level, and spiritual maturity) as well as being a reflection of their leadership. If congregations were not able to change as a "people of God," the church would be in disarray with each individual member doing "his thing" off in his corner. In writing his pastoral letters, Paul addresses the whole church so that the whole church body can progress. To the Corinthians he appeals for a unified corporate witness worthy of Jesus Christ. He asks that they join *together* "in unity of mind and thought" (I Corinthians 1:10, *NASB*). He wants the church to have a commonality around the gospel of our Lord.

There is, of course, a sense of always starting over when new people change the makeup of an organization. And we will need to be reminded of the basics from time to time. However, a church is not an organization that merely reflects people in their cultural context. It also reflects the God whom they serve. The church is not society's witness about God. It is God's witness to society. If we have to change to be that Biblical witness, then so be it.

When a young man joins the military, he soon learns that though he retains an individual identity, he is henceforth part of something larger than himself. He stands for what his unit, division, and ultimately his country stands for. As a member of an organization, he takes on its beliefs, policies, and methodology.

The corporate witness of a church can and should review its presuppositions from time to time as new people are added. But we need to teach in order to continue our collective "faith-walk" without having to regularly start all over again, as Sisyphus was condemned to do forever, pushing a huge boulder up the mountain only on nearing the top to have it roll down again. New people should see the music program as part of the developing corporate witness of a church and should make every effort to identify with what God has done in the past, is doing in the present, and will do in the future.

The church musician must use his creative ingenuity in evaluating his congregation's musical and spiritual tone. This will be more difficult than evaluating one of his musical ensembles. But the fact is that congregations do have a collective "average musical ability." They also must grow without arbitrary decisions as to how much growth is possible. The music director cannot sit back contented to do the same things over and over, using the excuse that new people make such a stationary program mandatory. This is the opposite of prophetic ministry.

It would be risky to spell out exactly how the Biblical themes developed in these pages might work together. They are capable of such infinite arrangement that to even hint at a standardized application would be to destroy the whole idea. There are no stock formulas to be applied mechanistically. There are only Biblical principles requiring creative insights for organizing them into a meaningful working counterpoint for a particular situation.

Nevertheless, we will attempt to organize our often contradictory themes into a suggested design to address what might be expected in a hypothetical church situation—"hypothetical" because every church is so unique that it is impossible to create an "average" church. We repeat, this must *not* be seen as *the* way that every music ministry will be affected by this working counterpoint. What we say about this hypothetical situation may well fit some churches, but it is not intended to be a model except in general procedure.

Writing, like melody, is linear. Music, however, has the advantage of being able to grant several melodies simultaneous existence in the same piece (hence counterpoint). Because writing deals with one sentence at a time, what follows will be a one-at-a-time written out application of each of these themes. In actual practice, however, they will be at work contrapuntally (i.e., several themes at once in beneficent balance). Some will, of course, be dominant at certain times, others at other times.

Because of the necessity for loving identification with this hypothetical congregation, we have chosen the incarnation to be the opening theme of our pastoral music ministry. That part of the doctrine which speaks of the immanence of God (His personal caring for the world) explains that immanence is demonstrated best by God's sending His Son to redeem us from sin. The key here is that God displayed to us—He demonstrated—His care by the action of sending the Son. He did not merely talk about love; He showed us.

In a ministry of music founded on Biblical principles, it is no less important for the music minister to demonstrate the love of Christ. He does this by taking on the servant role modeled for us by Jesus. Becoming one with the congregation as he serves them in *agape* love builds a bond of trust that is the bedrock of a prophetic music program.

The servant role of which we speak is best shown through the attitude, "What can I do to help?" Pastoral ministry at work here will show the music director to be an ardent under-shepherd of those entrusted to him, ministering to the sick, praying with the needy, and partying with the joyful. He will be a janitor when necessary, an errand boy if needed, a preacher if called upon. No task is too great or too small. He will be a "washer of feet." Jesus said it best: "If I do not wash you, you have no part with Me" (John 13:8, *NASB*). And again: "If I then, the Lord and the Teacher, washed your feet, you also ought to wash another's feet. For I gave you an example that you should also do as I do to you" (John 13:14-15, *NASB*). "Let the greatest among you become as the youngest, and the leader as one who serves" (Luke 22:26, *RSV*).

Even more important than doing the work of a servant is one's attitude when serving. There is no place for a proud spirit. A minister of music must serve without condescension, without malice, without resentment at having to perform tasks "beneath him." Paul's words clearly ring out:

> Having this attitude in yourself which was also in Christ Jesus, who, although He existed in the form of God, did not regard equality with God a thing to be grasped, but emptied Himself, taking the form of a bond-servant, and being made in the likeness of men. And being found in appearance as a man, He humbled Himself by being obedient to the point of death, even death on a cross. (Philippians 2:5-8, *NASB*).

A love such as this is patient and kind; it does not brag and is not arrogant; it does not act unbecomingly, does not take into account a wrong suffered; love bears all things. Love never fails.[9] This humility, love, and servanthood of our Lord is how we, acting for Him in the ministry of music, are to conduct ourselves.

Our main concern then in choosing music will be relevancy. The music done in worship will clearly reflect the congregation's musical vocabulary. This probably means that the general style of music and even the specific repertoire will not change much. Perhaps an entire year will go by before the music director and congregation are ready to launch into anything new; if the tradition of the congregation is to sing with bass guitar, mandolin, tambourine and piano, it will be kept that way. On the other hand, if the pipe organ is the only accompaniment to singing, rely on it. Keep the status quo, especially in musical style. Get to know and appreciate "their" music, "their" way of singing and playing, and "their" form of worship.

In drawing heavily from what has been done, we must be particularly careful to avoid things which in reality are too difficult. Keep the music simple in its technical requirements so that whatever is done is done thoroughly and well. Make time for fellowship and fun. Use the "light touch" in rehearsal.

Time must be made in rehearsal for building a caring, sharing, ministering community. A corporate sense of God's incarnate love must be instilled in the group as people open up to one another and to God. Under the leadership of the director, the choir can begin to see their music as ministry to the Lord—a response to Him for the new life He gives. As the vertical aspect of the God-man relationship is celebrated, the horizontal aspect of the man-to-man and choir-to-congregation relationship will come into play. Ministry is singing to God for the edification of the congregation of saints.

During the first year when we are stressing these aspects of our incarnation theme, there will be opportunity to lay the groundwork necessary for the introduction of the next theme: stewardship—"doing one's best." Every rehearsal is bound to have a moment or two when it would be appropriate to mention the theological call for using well whatever God gives us. Casual remarks will go far in making such a theme seem less foreign when the time comes to emphasize it.

When the director is fully confident that the incarnation theme has "taken hold" it is time to move to our second theme. A concept such as "doing one's best" is not foreign to churched people and is logical for introduction at this time. While we are developing this new theme in the music ministry of our hypothetical church, let us keep in mind that the incarnation theme continues to affect our stewardship emphasis in contrapuntal manner.

The most obvious application of "doing one's best" is in the rehearsal. Here one is faced continually with a corporate need for practicing until the optimum performance level is reached, or until there is no more time to rehearse. The optimum performance level is set not only by the boundaries of time and musical expertise, but also by the determination to use well the gifts God has given us. To urge people to give their best time, talent, and energy in learning a piece of music is a very natural utilization of the stewardship theme.

One can also utilize this Biblical principle when conducting congregational singing. The majority of churches sing half-heartedly. To offer that "sacrifice of praise" (as the writer of Hebrews 13:15 puts it) in collective testimony requires effort. Singing requires a stewardship of one's "musical praise ability." To offer to God a musical "worth-ship" with sloth and indifference is disrespectful and displeasing to God. The music director can lovingly admonish the believers to a more mature posture toward congregational singing by the use of this stewardship theme. He need not preach about it, but mentioning it at an appropriate moment will help encourage them to fulfill their musical-praise potential.

Other practical things such as being on time for rehearsals, the imperative of consistent rehearsal attendance, and taking seriously the leadership role of the choir in worship are all fairly obvious. When there are only sixty minutes of rehearsal time, good stewardship means using them to best advantage—and that can only be done when the choir is there in strength for the full hour. The stewardship of good preparation will lead to effective ministry during the service.

Personnel recruitment is another area that can be helped by this stewardship principle. In giving talent, God means for it to be used. Centering on this Biblical idea is a good way of enlisting people to help who have the necessary musical and spiritual qualifications. It is also a way of opening up new avenues of music ministry to people in the church who have unusual musical skills. Playing a musical saw may not be appropriate as a Sunday morning offertory, but it has the potential for demonstrating to the sixth-grade choir the principles of musical physics which are helpful in understanding the workings of musical instruments. We use to the utmost whomever and whatever God gives us.

In working out this theme, there inevitably will come a time when the choir and congregation will be ready for the next theme which focuses on the growth aspect of stewardship. This third theme is a very necessary corollary to "doing one's best," and is critical because it will serve as a transition to our creation theme, a theme which probably will be our first opportunity for prophetic ministry, directional balance, or simply put, change.

Both congregation and choir must fully understand the necessity for growth and the potential it has for leading us into new avenues of endeavor. The congregation needs to be informed of it indirectly, such as through the church newsletter (an editorial by the music director), through the Sunday bulletin, or perhaps from the pulpit. The choir, on the other hand, must be led very carefully and systematically to an understanding of the Biblical material on this subject.

The understanding of the choir must come first through teaching about growth (taking a few minutes from rehearsal or in a choir Sunday School class, et cetera) and second by participating in the growth process. That is, as they rationally learn about the stewardship of growth, they must in fact experience it. Such growth might begin with the mechanistic part of musicianship: sight-singing, vocal production, phrasing, and so on. Areas need to be chosen at first in which there is real opportunity for the choir singers themselves to apprehend the progress that is actually being made. Once they see that it can be done, there will be less and less need for them to continually monitor their own musical advancement. It is at this point (another year, perhaps) that the level of trust in what the music director is doing will be great enough to warrant breaking some new ground.

Growth in music will inevitably lead the choir along the path of maturing musical expression. We say "maturing" because we never arrive at maturity. There are always new musical expressions that continually challenge us. But one of the reasons we want to do new music is a Biblical one. We want to grow to reach the potential that God in His wisdom has given us. We want to have an increase to give to the Lord.

The question arises, "What new music?" Does the music director choose blindly or at random? Obviously if we are choosing music from a Biblical base rather than from an aesthetic or pragmatic one, we are naturally led to use the doctrine that has the most to do with music making. Remember, however, that we still have the themes of incarnation (relevance) and stewardship (doing one's best and growth) concurrent in the music ministry fabric. They will still influence what we do and how we do it.

Our fourth and fifth themes are closely related. The doctrine of creation tells us that man's creating should be guided by universal artistic norms inherent in creation and should break new ground with imagination and integrity. The broad *Imago Dei* emphasizes that everyone has some ability to fulfill responsibly the creation and cultural mandates. Choice of music will be heavily influenced by what these doctrines say to us.

The time has come, then, for the music director to exercise his gift of discernment and choose musical pieces which can stand the scrutiny of a thorough creative (artistic) examination. He brings into play his knowledge of music theory (melody, harmony, counterpoint, form, and so on) and makes a judgment as to musical worth. Those pieces which can clearly be labeled as meeting the requirements of a Biblical creativity (artistry if you will) then become candidates for inclusion in the repertoire. It must be taken for granted, of course, that text, difficulty level, and appropriateness will have already been analyzed.

The personnel in the music program need to be apprised of the normality of such a creative music. It should be shown that being responsible for the creation mandate is no idle theory. Furthermore, they need to understand that creativity begins with composition, passes through performance, and ends with listening. All musical activity needs the creative spark.

Composition, however, is probably the biggest problem in establishing a creative music ministry. Often a particular style of music has, as part of its stylistic identity, an inseparable bond to noncreativity. If it were creative it would no longer be that style, but would be something different. One cannot always find creative music in one's favorite style, in which case a better alternative must be found.

Truthfully, the participants in the music program are usually not equipped to make such musical judgments. This is to be expected, of course. What they do need is to believe that their director is competent as well as caring. His choices will not be based on whim or personal likes, but on musical knowledge and intuition. Their understanding that his choices musically reflect the creatorship of God through men (*creatio continua*) will give a nobility and dignity to the process which is often missing.

Musicians, as well as the congregation as a whole, should know that musical value or creative worth is something that can be measured, even though it is not an exact science. The widespread notion that value is purely subjective is, as noted in Chapter 2, a most insidious deception. When musical value is thought to be nothing more than personal taste, Biblical music ministry is impossible. It is impossible because creativity is taken out from under normal authoritative Biblical norms (unity, variety, coherence, truth, imagination, and so on) and dissolved into an absurdist view in which every man assigns "value" according to his own personal choice and desire. Hence it is entirely possible to have the same music be both "good" and "bad," "creative" and "uncreative." These terms, supposed opposites, become meaningless when they are used to describe the same thing. A world-view in which every man does what is right in his own eyes produces moral, ethical, social, and artistic chaos. It is, as we have already said, not an option for the Christian.

The contrapuntal conversation with the other three concurrent themes is bound to create a certain amount of intense "discussion." It may well be that in our hypothetical church, creative music will be in tension with the actual musical vocabulary of the congregation. A dialogue between the necessity for relevance and the necessity for creativity then ensues. What the minister of music needs to do is become a teacher so that the gap between "their" music and "creative" music or between incarnation and creation is lessened. He does not foist his ideas on people; he shepherds them.

Here, then, can be seen the Biblical music ministry in action. Rather than dumping a whole new set of musical rules on the church, the director carefully leads the church toward more mature musical expressions. Perhaps a new piece with good musical qualifications will be incorporated infrequently at first (four times a year) but with increasing frequency until the church has gone as far as it can go, taking into account the background, cultural environment, and education of the congregation. The themes of incarnation, stewardship, creation, and the broad *Imago Dei* will provide the music minister with goals, methodological instruction, psychological satisfaction, and above all, Biblical rationale.

A host of other topics inherent in the doctrine of creation and the broad *Imago Dei* could be mentioned: the use of music from the past, church nurture of creativity, the use of creative gifts in Christian education, and others. After all, the only limit to our creativity is the boundless imagination given to us by the Creator.

In determining the music used for stressing creativity, music that we want to be understood by the people of our hypothetical church, we can be helped by the inclusion of a sixth theme, that of faith—living life in the Christian faith. Here we see life as a unified whole—a holistic life that worships unreservedly, emotionally, and intellectually.

Finding such music for our church takes thought, careful scrutiny, and patience. The congregation of which we speak needs music, let us say, from the common practice period that is rich in emotive design and compositionally creative. Therefore music with accelerandos, ritards, dynamic contrasts, carefully controlled crescendos and diminuendos, unusually placed accents, and an emphasis on the melodic line with rich harmonic accompaniment narrows down one's search to some type of romantic composition. Having the intellectual side (technical craftsmanship) to consider will help keep our musical choices from being maudlin, sentimental, or emotionalistic. Worship through such a music will incorporate the whole man, both in performing and in listening.

If certain congregations are less emotional, music can be found that also fits them. And if they are devoid of any role of the intellect in worship, emotionalism being the norm, then the music director can teach them to open the whole man to God.

Choice of music will avoid anything that is too far ahead of the congregation. Music that sounds like gibberish, because it is so cerebral will be avoided until such time as people can understand it and have a feeling identification with it. This particular aspect of the faith principle helps guard against our moving too far afield in one's quest for creative worship music, for worship takes place best when there is both feeling and understanding.

Ultimately a maturing ministry of music must face up to the subject of musical witness. Several new themes, each dealing with the some special aspect of musical witness, will now be introduced in turn. These themes are: the narrow *Imago Dei,* incarnation—form and content, and the Gospel as embodied in church music.

No subject in these pages is more momentous than the seventh theme, the narrow *Imago Dei.* Here we see the church music program as a collective musical testimony of the fact that we "image" a creator. The verb "to image" takes on a special potency as we realize that in our music we show the world what we think of our God. Our music speaks for us louder than our words. When banality, mediocrity, and cliché-ridden compositions dominate our musical program, the God we image forth is an uncreative entity. This is not to say that the church musician can ever hope to have a high enough musical image of God to match Him as He is. That is unthinkable. What we ask of our musicians is that they reflect the best creativity that God has given to us. We are not called to do any more than this.

Responsibility for imaging a God of integrity belongs to every member of the music program. After the doctrine of the *Imago Dei* has been assimilated, we are no longer concerned with whether our music will be accepted but with how our music reflects the creativity of God.

Another aspect of musical witness is our eighth theme, incarnation—form and content. Our concern here is that we see the music we do as an analogue of the gospel, that is as a musical expression that implicitly incarnates general gospel content. The gospel action and the musical form will bear one another out. The integrity of the gospel message found in the words will be matched by a like integrity in the musical form.

Closely tied to form and content is our ninth theme, that of musically embodying the gospel. We are particularly concerned here that the pervasive features of mass culture be avoided in our musical expressions, because these traits are so unlike the gospel. The musical embodiment of our general culture is pop music. As a musical form, "pop" mirrors the world, and for this reason it should be avoided at this point. Instead, church music should exhibit the values of honesty, discipline, and creativity. In a sense, the musical form is the "show and tell" of the gospel. If the form is not conformable to the intent of the message it is confusing to use it.

The music director in our hypothetical church is going to have a difficult time persuading his musicians and congregation to take musical witness seriously, particularly in this matter of gospel pop, because pop culture, in the widest sense, is the most influential factor in the average church-goer's musical makeup. His appreciation and understanding of musical things is the result of his being continually bombarded by radio, television, and recorded pop music.

As a teacher, the church musician will be faced with a real challenge here. He cannot succumb to any private wish to follow the crowd and be a pleaser of men, nor can he alienate the church from his ministry by arbitrarily doing what he knows he should. The counterpoint here between these witness themes and the incarnation and stewardship themes will help him to be musically understanding, yet firm; adaptable, yet having a creative vision. It may be years before a congregation can honestly be convinced of the need to shun that which is made poorly for the express purpose of becoming popular, and perhaps some congregations will never reach this level. Yet we always try, keeping in mind the need to be prophetic.

Faith-action is the tenth theme to be included in the philosophical counterpoint of our hypothetical church. Here we address the subject of tendency gratification—of seeing life as an adventurous journey complete with risks as we travel from horizon to horizon. We practice life as a faith-walk—faith being "the substance of things hoped for, the evidence of things not seen" (Hebrews 11:1, *KJV*).

We invite the choir and congregation to join us in such a musical faith-walk by the utilization of not only creative music, but music that is unfamiliar, perhaps having a style twist to it that leaves us feeling puzzled, not knowing how it will progress or end, ambiguous to a fault. Such music is a description of life based on faith, a repudiation that religion is a security blanket under which nice people get comfortable.

The music director may not have as difficult a time in teaching his people this musical doctrine as might be expected. Living as a "pilgrim" is fairly common imagery, and living the faith-life is seen as a needed goal in every Christian experience. When music is translated into a representation of how we should live life, there might well be an immediate identification with the intent of that music, but only if there has been sufficient teaching and explanation.

This particular subject is important to those churches that may have had a good background of creative music of one style period only. The time comes when we must pull up stakes and go on. Musically, this could be twentieth-century avant-garde electronic music, or a musical style such as that of Jean Berger, or a musical adventure into the sixteenth century. If we never move from our self-satisfied position, we repudiate our faith principle.

The last theme to be woven into our contrapuntal web of themes for our hypothetical church is the transcendency of God, the *mysterium tremendum,* the mystery and awe inherent in the contemplation of the Holy, His unknowableness, and His awesomeness. It takes a certain spiritual maturity to realize that we cannot own God, that we can only know of Him what He chooses to reveal, and that He is fundamentally apart and different from man. To know of His "set-apart-ness" and His holiness is an important step in showing Him the respect He is due.

One can see why this theme is necessary. In an age that stresses immanence, often a radical immanence in which God is thought of as a genie to do our bidding or a pet rock to decorate our lives, the transcendency of God puts in balance the truth of His "hereness." God is both immanent and transcendent.

The music that reinforces these ideas will, of course, be different for each individual congregation. For the congregation of our hypothetical church we will use a music of integrity with an emphasis on the open harmony of the early fifteenth century. Gregorian melodies also have a pathos and restrained character that lend themselves to describing transcendency musically. Certain twentieth-century styles will also be appropriate.

Such music is exactly the opposite of the now-generation-gospel-pop which is so much in vogue. Stressing mystery and awe may be another tack for getting congregations and choirs to occasionally use music other than the pop genre. If we try new music for Biblical reasons, Christian people should make the attempt to give it a fair hearing.

Many more themes from our major topics could be developed and included in our counterpoint. But enough has been said to give us a glimmer of methodological insight as to how these topics from God's Word can help in the opening up of a responsible music ministry.

When we have woven this contrapuntal design theme by theme over a period of years, it is necessary to keep in mind the entire design when contemplating a particular decision. We must practice "listening" to what each has to say to us as new problems and opportunities arise from day to day. Our obligation is to stress the one that seems the most important at the time without forgetting the importance of the others.

The *interplay* between the separate truths of these theological themes produces "the truth" foundational to music ministry, a truth both accommodating and prophetic. Perhaps the best picture we have of such theological musical situationalism is God's initial invitation and subsequent plan for each of us. We see Jesus with open and everloving arms unconditionally calling all men unto himself. But after regeneration we are called to a continual life process of being conformed to the image of the Son. We come as we are, but are expected to change, caterpillars who are to evolve into butterflies, babes who are to grow into adulthood.

Ministry should be characterized by both of these distinctions—an unconditional acceptance of our people as they are and a passionate desire to teach them God's full intention for the redeemed. It is necessary that the music director avoid the pitfalls of choosing only one side of the truth or of falsely separating the spiritual from the musical, the content from the form. If he has the correct Biblical motivation and is listening to the prophetic voice of these theological themes, the pastoral musician can be confident that in being a servant of his congregation he is ultimately the servant of God.

The key is an unquenchable and persistent vision of the marvelous contrapuntal design for music and ministry found in God's Word. Let the dynamic of this counterpoint be both rationally understood and warmly felt. Let it be the genesis for a joyful pilgrimage to new horizons.

NOTES TO CHAPTER 1   PHILOSOPHICAL PERSPECTIVES

1. *Music in Church: Report of the Archbishops' Committee,* Noel T. Hopkins, chairman, (Westminster, S.W.I.: Church Information Office, 1960), p. 6.

2. Archibald T. Davison, *Protestant Church Music in America* (Boston: E.C. Schirmer Music Co., 1948), pp. 94-142.

3. DeWitt Henry Parker, *The Principles of Aesthetics* (New York: F.S. Crofts and Co., 1946), p. 297.

4. Charles T. Smith, *Music and Reason* (New York: Social Sciences Pub., 1948), pp. 151-152.

5. David Elton Trueblood, *Philosophy of Religion* (New York: Harper and Row, 1957), pp. 118ff.

6. Gunnar C. Urang, *Church Music—For the Glory of God* (Moline, Ill.: Christian Service Foundation, 1956), p. 5.

7. W. Hines Sims, "What is Good Church Music?" *Church Musician* 2 No. 11 (1951): p. 12.

8. Trueblood, *Philosophy of Religion,* p. 41.

9. Erik Routley, *The Church and Music* (London: Gerald Duckworth and Co. Ltd., 1967), p. 227; *Church Music and Theology* (Philadelphia: Fortress Press, 1965), pp. 12ff.

NOTES TO CHAPTER 2   THE DOCTRINE OF CREATION

1. Langdon Gilkey, *Maker of Heaven and Earth,* Anchor Books (Garden City, N.Y.: Doubleday and Co., 1965), p. 4

2. Robert Bruce McLaren "The Threat of Aestheticism," *Christianity Today,* 7 November 1960, p. 16.

3. Peter A. Bertocci, "Free Will, The Creativity of God, and Order," *Current Philosophical Issues: Essays in Honor of Curt John Ducasse,* ed. Frederick C. Dommeyer (Springfield, Ill.: Charles C. Thomas, 1966), p. 229.

4. Gilkey, *Maker of Heaven and Earth,* pp. 65, 120.

5. John Kobler, "Everything We Do Is Music, " *Saturday Evening Post,* 19 October 1968, p. 46.

6. Ragnar Bring, "The Gospel of the New Creation," *Dialog* 3 (Autumn 1964: p. 275.

7. Leonard Verduin, *Somewhat Less Than God: The Biblical View of Man* (Grand Rapids: Wm. B. Eerdmans Pub. Co., 1970), p. 27.

8. Arthur F. Holmes, "The Idea of a Christian College," *Christianity Today,* 31 July 1970, p. 6.

9. Emil Brunner, *The Divine Imperative,* trans. Olive Wyon (Philadelphia: Westminster Press, 1947), p. 484.

10. W. Paul Jones, "Art as the Creator of Lived Meaning," *Journal of Bible and Religion* 31 (1963): p. 229.

11. George F. Thomas, "Central Christian Affirmations," *The Christian Answer,* ed. Henry P. Van Dusen (New York: Charles Scribner's Sons, 1945), p. 104.

12. Paul Waitman Hoon, *The Integrity of Worship* (New York: Abingdon Press, 1971), pp. 96-97.

13. Carl Schalk, "The Shape of Church Music in the '70s," *Journal of Church Music* 13 (1971): p. 17.

14. T.S. Eliot, "The Sacred Wood." *Tradition and the Individual Talent,* London: Methuen and Company Ltd., 6th edition, 1948, and quoted in James Johnson Sweeney, "The Literary Artist and the Other Arts," *Spiritual Problems in Contemporary Literature*, ed. Stanley Romaine Hopper, Harper Torchbooks/The Cloister Library (New York: Harper and Bros., 1957), p. 7.

15. Gordon Jacob, *The Composer and His Art* (New York: Oxford University Press, 1955), p. 3.

16. Edgar Wind, *Art and Anarchy* (New York: Alfred A. Knopf, 1965), p. 69.

17. Archie J. Bahm, "Creativity through Interdependence," *Southwestern Journal of Philosophy* 1 (Spring-Summer, 1970): p. 33.

18. Wind, *Art and Anarchy,* p. 68.

19. Constance F. Parvey, "Christian Art in Mid-Century," *Response* 9 (1968): p. 112.

20. Herman Berlinski, "In Search of Criteria," *American Guild of Organists Quarterly* 10 (April 1965): p. 76.

21. H. Grady Davis, "Worship Music in a Synthetic Culture," *Concordia Theological Monthly* 33 (1963): p. 737.

22. G. William Jones, *Sunday Night at the Movies* (Richmond, Va.: John Knox Press, 1968), p. 40.

NOTES TO CHAPTER 3   THE *IMAGO DEI*

1. Edmond Jacob, *Theology of the Old Testament,* trans. Arthur W. Heathcote and Phillip J. Allcock (New York: Harper and Bros. Pub., 1958), pp. 169-170.

2. Emil Brunner, *The Christian Doctrine of Creation and Redemption,* trans. Olive Wyon (London: Lutterwoth Press, 1952), p. 67.

3. Franklin Sherman, "God as Creative Artist," *Dialog* 3 (1964): p. 287.

4. Dorothy Sayers, *The Mind of the Maker* (Westport, Conn.: Greenwood Press, Pub., 1941), p. 22.

5. Emmanuel Chapman, *Saint Augustine's Philosophy of Beauty* (New York: Sheed and Ward, 1939), p. 77.

6. G.C. Berkouwer, *Man: The Image of God* (Grand Rapids: Wm. B. Eerdmans Pub. Co., 1962), p. 102.

7. Joseph H. Lookstein, "How Achieve a Sacred Image of Man?," *What is the Nature of Man?,* Religious Education Association (Philadelphia: Christian Education Press, 1959), p. 182.

8. Berkouwer, *Man: The Image of God,* p. 55.

9. W. Paul Jones, "Art as the Creator of Lived Meaning," *Journal of Bible and Religion* 31 (1963): p. 228.

10. Edith Schaeffer, *Hidden Art* (Wheaton, Ill.: Tyndale House Pub., 1972), p. 32.

11. Ibid., p.28.

12. Robert A. Cook, "That New Religious Music, " *Moody Monthly,* April 1977, p. 40.

NOTES TO CHAPTER 4   THE INCARNATION

1. Constance F. Parvey, "Christian Art in Mid-Century," *Response* 9 (Epiphany 1968): p. 109.

2. Text adapted from *A Hymn of the Nativity* by Richard Crashaw in the anthem, "Summer in Winter," by Robert N. Roth (Cincinatti: Canyon Press, 1958).

3. F.W. Dillistone, *Dramas of Salvation* (New York: Morehouse-Barlow Co., 1967), p.95.

4. Calvin Seerveld, *A Christian Critique of Art and Literature* (Toronto: Association for Reformed Scientific Studies, 1968), p. 17.

5. Eugene L. Brand, "Congregational Song: The Popular Music of the Church," *Church Music* (1968-1): p. 3.

6. Peter Allen, "The Problem of Communication," *English Church Music* (Croydon, England: Royal School of Church Music, 1966), p. 31.

7. Ron Goulart, *The Sword Swallower* (Garden City, N. Y.: Doubleday and Company, 1968), p. 104.

8. G. William Jones, *Sunday Night at the Movies* (Richmond, Va.: John Knox Press, 1968), pp. 48-49.

9. See E.J. Tinsley in "The Incarnation and Art," *The Church and the Arts,* ed. F.J. Glendenning (London: SCM Press Ltd., 1960), p. 21.

NOTES TO CHAPTER 5   THE GOSPEL AND CONTEMPORARY CULTURE

1. Dietrich Bonhoeffer, *The Cost of Discipleship* (New York: Macmillan Co., 1961), p. 36.

2. Op. Cit.

3. Ernest van den Haag, "A Dissent from the Consensual Society," *Culture for the Millions?,* ed. Norman Jacobs (Boston: Beacon Press, 1964), pp. 58-60.

4. Denys Thompson, ed., *Discrimination and Popular Culture* (Baltimore: Penguin Books, 1964), p. 12.

5. Bernard Rosenberg, "Mass Culture in America" *Mass Culture,* ed. Bernard Rosenberg and David Manning White (Glencoe, Ill.: Free Press, 1957), p. 10.

6. Paul Hindemith, *A Composer's World* (Cambridge: Harvard University Press, 1952), pp. 211-212.

7. Carl Halter, *God and Man in Music* (St. Louis: Concordia Pub. House, 1963), p. 11.

8. John A.T. Robinson, *The New Reformation* (Philadelphia: Westminster Press, 1965), pp. 48-50.

9. E. Clinton Gardner, *The Church as a Prophetic Community* (Philadelphia: Westminster Press, 1967), p. 182.

10. Edwin Liehmohn, *The Chorale* (Philadelphia: Muhlenberg Press, 1953), p. 12.

11. Eric Blom, ed., *Grove's Dictionary of Music and Musicians,* Vol. 1, 5th ed. (New York: St. Martin's Press, Inc., 1966), p. 848.

12. André Hodeir, *Toward Jazz* (New York: Grove Press, 1962), p. 200.

13. Hindemith, *A Composer's World,* p. 126.

14. David Ewen, *History of Popular Music* (New York: Barnes and Noble Inc., 1961), p. 157.

15. Paul S. Carpenter, *Music, An Art and A Business* (Norman: University of Oklahoma Press, 1950), p. 27.

16. Donald Hughes, "Recorded Music," *Discrimination and Popular Culture,* p. 154.

17. T.W. Adorno in "On Popular Music," *Studies in Philosophy and Social Science* 9, p. 17 and quoted in Robert William Miller, *The Christian Encounters the World of Pop Music and Jazz* (St. Louis: Concordia Pub. House, 1965), p. 54.

18. Harry S. Broudy, "Educational Theory and the Music Curriculum," *Perspectives in Music Education,* ed. Bonnie C. Kowall (Washington, D.C.: Music Educators National Conference, 1966), p. 179.

19. F.J. Glendenning, *The Church and the Arts* (London: SCM Press Ltd., 1960), p. 24.

20. Routley, *Church Music and Theology,* p. 37.

21. Roger Hazelton, *A Theological Approach to Art* (Nashville: Abingdon Press, 1967), p. 91.

22. Arthur Korb, *How to Write Songs That Sell* (Boston: Plymouth Publishing Co., 1957), p. 8.

23. Henry Boye, *How To Make Money Selling the Songs You Write* (New York: Frederick Fell Inc., 1970), p. 37.

24. Korb, *How To Write Songs That Sell,* p. 8.

25. Stuart Hall and Paddy Whannel, *The Popular Arts* (Boston: Beacon Press, 1967), p. 311.

26. See David Wilkerson, *The Devil's Heartbeat: Rock and Roll!* (Philipsburg, Pa.: Teen-Age Evangelism, n.d.).

27. Kurt Kaiser, "The Trends of Performance in the New Music," *The Music Journal of the Southern Baptist Church Music Conference* 5 (1973): p. 37.

28. Roy Harris, "Folk Songs," *A History and Encyclopedia of Country, Western and Gospel Music,* ed. Linnell Gentry (Nashville: Clairmont Corp., 1969), p. 99.

29. Ralph Vaughn Williams, *National Music* (London: Oxford University Press, 1963), p. 75.

30. Routley, *Church Music and Theology,* p. 106.

31. André Hodeir, *Jazz: Its Evolution and Essence,* trans. by David Noakes (New York: Grove Press, Inc., 1961), p. 24.

32. Leonard Bernstein, *The Joy of Music* (New York: Simon and Schuster, 1959), p. 118.

33. Hodier, *Toward Jazz,* p. 202.

34. Miller, *The Christian Encounters the World of Pop Music and Jazz* p. 105.

35. Hymn by W.A. Ogden in *Popular Hymns* (C.C. Cline and Co., 1883), p. 118.

NOTES TO CHAPTER 6   FAITH

1. Quoted by George Gordh in *Christian Faith and Its Cultural Expression* (Englewood Cliffs, N.J.: Prentice-Hall, Inc., 1962), p. 5.

2. Paul Henry Lang, "The *Patrimonium Musicae Sacrae* and the Task of Sacred Music Today," *Sacred Music*, 93 (1966-67): p. 126.

3. Frank Tirro, "Choral Music," *Choral Journal* 7 (September-October 1967): p. 20.

4. John Macquarrie, "What is the Gospel?" *Expository Times* 81 (1970): p. 299.

5. Charles R. Hoffer, *The Understanding of Music* (Belmont, Cal.: Wadsworth Pub. Co., 1967), p. 18.

6. Winfred Douglas, *Church Music in History and Practice*, (New York: Charles Scribner's Sons, 1937), p. 8.

7. Quoted by Deryck Cooke, *The Language of Music* (London: Oxford University Press, 1959), p. 11.

8. Aaron Copland, *What to Listen for in Music*, Mentor Book (New York: McGraw-Hill Book Co., 1957), p. 163.

9. Charles T. Smith, *Music and Reason* (New York: Social Sciences Pub., 1948), p. 20.

10. Paul Waitman Hoon, *The Integrity of Worship* (New York: Abingdon Press, 1971), p. 212.

11. Christopher Dearnley, "The Need for a Reformed Approach to Church Music," *English Church Music* (Croydon, England: Royal School of Church Music, 1969), p. 27.

12. Paul Henry Lang, "The Musician's Point of View," *Music* 2 (1968): p. 36.

13. Denis Stevens and Alec Robertson, eds., *The Pelican History of Music, I: Ancient Forms to Polyphony* (Baltimore: Penguin Books, 1960), p. 284.

14. Archibald T. Davidson and Willi Apel, *Historical Anthology of Music*, Vol. 1 (Cambridge: Harvard University Press, 1959), p. 220.

15. Albert Seay, *Music in the Medieval World* (Englewood Cliffs, N.J.: Prentice-Hall, Inc., 1965), p. 127.

16. Imogene Horsley, *Fugue: History and Practice* (New York: Free Press, 1966), p. 1.

17. James Higgs, *Fugue* (New York: H.W. Gray Co.), p. 78.

18. Julius Portnoy, *Music in the Life of Man* (New York: Holt, Rinehart and Winston, 1963), p. 48.

19. Paul Hindemith, *A Composer's World*, pp. 14-22.

20. Op. Cit.

21. Ibid., p. 126: This is a scathing attack on musical standardization.

22. Ibid., p. 19.

23. Erik Routley, "The Vocabulary of Church Music," *Union Seminary Quarterly Review* 18 (1963): 142.

24. Carl Halter, *God and Man in Music* (St. Louis: Concordia Pub. House, 1963), p. 73.

25. Hebrews 11:8-9 KJV.

26. David Elton Trueblood, *Philosophy of Religion* (New York: Harper and Row, 1957), p. 27.

27. Routley, *Music Sacred and Profane* (London: Independent Press Ltd., 1960), p. 139.

28. Cadences are points of relative harmonic repose, each of which concludes the respective building blocks of a musical composition (from the smaller phrase to the larger section), and which ultimately brings to an end the completed composition. The cadences of a piece are the ''goals'' which tonal music utilizes to establish its architectural progress.

29. Leonard Meyer, ''Some Remarks on Value and Greatness in Music,'' *Aesthetic Inquiry: Essays on Art Criticism and the Philosophy of Art,* eds., Monroe C. Beardsley and Herbert M. Schueller (Belmont, Cal.: Dickenson Pub. Co., Inc., 1967), p. 263.

30. Herman Berlinski, ''Pop, Rock and Sacred,'' II, *Music* 5 (1971): p. 48.

31. Leonard B. Meyer, ''Some Remarks on Value and Greatness in Music,'' p. 178.

NOTES TO CHAPTER 7   STEWARDSHIP

1. Elizabeth O'Conner, *Eighth Day of Creation* (Waco, Texas.: Word Books, 1971), p. 13.

2. Alvin Porteous, *The Search for Christian Credibility* (New York: Abingdon Press, 1969), p. 172.

3. Quoted from Hoon, *The Integrity of Worship,* p. 186.

4. Frederick K. Wentz, ''Lay Theology—A Synopsis,'' *My Job and My Faith,* ed. Wentz (New York: Abingdon Press, 1967), p. 184.

5. Ibid., p. 186.

6. T. Glyn Thomas, ''The Relationship of Art to Religion: A Study of John Ruskin,'' *Expository Times* 82 (1971): p. 182.

7. John S. McMullen, *Stewardship Unlimited* (Richmond, Va.: John Knox Press, 1966), p. 81.

8. H.R. Rookmaaker, ''Letter to a Christian Artist,'' *Christianity Today,* 2 September (1966): p. 25.

9. Carl Schalk, ''The Dilemma of the Contemporary Composer of Church Music,'' *Response* 7 (1965): p. 77.

10. Heinrich Bornkamm, *The Heart of Reformation Faith,* trans. John W. Doberstein (New York: Harper and Row, 1965), p. 116.

11. Russell Coleburt, *The Search for Values* (New York: Sheed and Ward, 1960), p. 69.

12. Taken from Walter E. Buszin, ''Luther's Quotes on Music, '' *Journal of Church Music* 13 (1971): p. 5.

13. Derek Kidner, *The Christian and the Arts* (Chicago: Inter-Varisty Press, 1961), p. 11.

14. Robert Stone Tangeman, ''Religion and the Arts: II, Music and the Church,'' *Union Seminary Quarterly Review* 12 (1957): p. 56.

15. Arthur B. Hunkins, ''The Serious Contemporary Composer and the Church Today,'' *Music Ministry* 2 (1970): p. 13.

16. Robert Elmore, ''The Place of Music in Christian Life,'' *Christianity Today,* 31 January 1964, p. 8.

NOTES TO CHAPTER 8   MYSTERY AND AWE

1. Emil Brunner, *Our Faith,* trans. by John W. Rilling (New York: Charles Scribner's Sons, n.d.), p. 11.

2. Heinrich Bornkamm, *The Heart of Reformation Faith,* p. 101. The form of this quotation is mine.

3. Bornkamm, *The Heart of Reformation Faith,* p. 102

4. Nancy E. Sartin, ''Toward a Musician's Theology, '' *Response* 7 (1965): p. 9.

5. Henry Grady Davis, ''Theology in Relation to Arrangements for Music in the Church,'' *Response* 3 (1961): p. 5.

6. Van Cliburn, ''Great Music a Gift from God,'' *Arts in Religion,* 19 (1969): p. 3.

7. Calvin Seerveld, *A Christian Critique of Art and Literature* (Toronto: Association for Reformed Scientific Studies, 1968), p. 29.

8. Carl Halter has written with particular clarity on this matter of meaning, mystery, and truth in *God and Man in Music* (St. Louis: Concordia Pub. House, 1963) and in ''Church Music as Art and Witness,'' *Journal of Church Music* 5 (1963): pp. 2-5.

9. Halter, ''Church Music as Art and Witness,'' p. 3.

10. Op. Cit.

11. Michael Tippett, ''A Child of Our Time,'' *The Composer's Point of View: Essays on Twentieth-Century Choral Music by Those Who Wrote It,* ed. Robert Stephan Hines (Norman: University of Oklahoma Press, 1963), p. 113. The brackets belong to Tippett.

12. Austin C. Lovelace and William C. Rice, *Music and Worship in the Church* (Nashville: Abingdon Press, 1960), p. 15.

13. Herman Berlinski, ''Pop, Rock and Sacred,'' Part II, *Music* 5 (1971): p. 49.

NOTES TO CHAPTER 9   CONCLUSION

1. Emil Brunner, *The Christian Doctrine of Creation and Redemption,* trans. Olive Wyon (London: Lutterworth Press, 1952), p. 363.

2. Amos Wilder, ''The Arts as Interpreters of the Modern World,'' *Encounter* 28 (Autumn 1967): p. 306.

3. Erik Routley, *Church Music and Theology* (Philadelphia: Fortress Press, 1965), p. 56.

4. J. Robert Nelson, ''Emil Brunner,'' *A Handbook of Christian Theologians,* edited Dean G. Peerman and Martin E. Marty (New York: World Pub. Co., 1965), pp. 416-417.

5. Emil Brunner, *The Divine Imperative,* trans. Olive Wyon (Philadelphia: Westminster Press, 1950), p. 500.

6. Robert W. Wood, ''The Aesthetic—A Forgotten Aspect of the Christian Life,'' *Japan Christian Quarterly* 28 (January 1962): p. 36.

7. Walter Piston, *Counterpoint* (W.W. Norton and Co., New York, 1947), p. 9.

9. J. Edward Moyer, ''Convocation Lecture Series by Dr. Erik Routley,'' *News and Notes,* June 1970, pp. 1-2, 6-8.

10. Excerpts from I Corinthians 13:4-8, NASB.

SELECTED BIBLIOGRAPHY

BOOKS

Berkouwer, G.C. *Man: The Image of God.* Grand Rapids: Wm. B. Eerdmans Pub. Co., 1962.

Berstein, Leonard. *The Joy of Music.* New York: Simon and Schuster, 1959.

Bertocci, Peter A. "Free Will, The Creativity of God, and Order." *Current Philosophical Issues: Essays in Honor of Curt John Ducasse.* Edited by Frederick C. Dommeyer. Springfield, Ill.: Charles C. Thomas, 1966.

Blom, Eric, ed. *Groves Dictionary of Music and Musicians.* 5th ed. New York: St. Martin's Press, Inc., 1966.

Bonhoeffer, Dietrich. *The Cost of Discipleship*. Revised ed. New York: Macmillan Co., 1961.

Bornkamm, Heinrich. *The Heart of Reformation Faith.* Translated by John W. Doberstein. New York: Harper and Row, 1965.

Boye, Henry. *How to Make Money Selling the Songs You Write.* New York: Frederick Fell Inc., 1970.

Broudy, Harry S. "Educational Theory and the Music Curriculum." *Perspectives in Music Education.* Edited by Bonnie C. Kowall. Washington, D.C.: Music Educators National Conference, 1966.

Brunner, Emil. *The Divine Imperative.* Translated by Olive Wyon. Philadelphia: Westminster Press, 1947.

_____. *Dogmatics.* Vol.2: *The Christian Doctrine of Creation and Redemption.* Translated by Olive Wyon. London: Lutterworth Press, 1952.

_____. *Our Faith.* Translated by John W. Rilling. New York: Charles Scribner's Sons, n.d.

Carpenter, Paul S. *Music, An Art and A Business.* Norman: University of Oklahoma Press, 1950.

Chapman, Emmanuel. *Saint Augustine's Philosophy of Beauty.* New York: Sheed and Ward, 1939.

Coleburt, Russel. *The Search for Values.* New York: Sheed and Ward, 1960.

Cooke, Deryck. *The Language of Music.* London: Oxford University Press, 1959.

Copland, Aaron. *What to Listen for in Music.* Mentor Books. New York: McGraw-Hill Book Co., 1957.

Davison, Archibald T. *Protestant Church Music in America.* Boston: E.C. Schirmer Music Co., 1948.

Dillistone, F.W. *Dramas of Salvation.* New York: Morehouse-Barlow Co., 1967.

Douglas, Winfred. *Church Music in History and Practice.* New York: Charles Scribner's Sons, 1937.

Ewen, David. *History of Popular Music.* New York: Barnes and Noble Inc., 1961.

Gardner, E. Clinton. *The Church as a Prophetic Community.* Philadelphia: Westminster Press, 1967.

Gilkey, Langdon. *Maker of Heaven and Earth.* Anchor Books. Garden City, N.Y.: Doubleday and Co., 1965.

Glendenning, F.J., ed. *The Church and the Arts.* London: SCM Press Ltd., 1960.

Gordh, George. *Christian Faith and Its Cultural Expression*. Englewood Cliffs, N.J.: Prentice-Hall, Inc., 1962.

Goulart, Ron. *The Sword Swallower*. Garden City, N.Y.: Doubleday and Co., 1968.

Hall, Stuart and Whannel, Paddy. *The Popular Arts*. Boston: Beacon Press, 1967.

Halter, Carl. *God and Man in Music*. St. Louis: Concordia Pub. House, 1963.

Harris, Roy. "Folk Songs." *A History and Encyclopedia of Country Western and Gospel Music*. edited by Linnell Gentry. Nashville: Clairmont Corp., 1969.

Hazelton, Roger. *A Theological Approach to Art*. Nashville: Abingdon Press, 1967.

Hindemith, Paul. *A Composer's World*. Cambridge: Harvard University Press, 1952.

Hines, Robert Stephen, ed. *The Composer's Point of View: Essays on Twentieth-Century Choral Music by Those Who Wrote It*. Norman: University of Oklahoma Press, 1963.

Hodeir, André. *Jazz: Its Evolution and Essence*. Translated by David Noakes. New York: Grove Press, Inc., 1961.

———. *Toward Jazz*. New York: Grove Press, Inc., 1962.

Hoon, Paul Waitman. *The Integrity of Worship*. Nashville: Abingdon Press, 1971.

Horsley, Imogene. *Fugue: History and Practice*. New York: Free Press, 1966.

Hughes, Donald. "Recorded Music." *Discrimination and Popular Culture*. Edited by Denys Thompson. Baltimore: Penguin Books, 1964.

Jacob, Edmond. *Theology of the Old Testament*. Translated by Arthur W. Heathcote and Phillip J. Allcock. New York: Harper and Bros. Pub., 1958.

Jacob, Gordon. *The Composer and His Art*. New York: Oxford University Press, 1955.

Jacobs, Norman, ed. *Culture for the Millions?* Boston: Beacon Press, 1964.

Jones, G. William. *Sunday Night at the Movies*. Richmond, Va.: John Knox Press, 1968.

Kidner, Derek. *The Christian and the Arts*. Chicago: Inter-Varsity Press, 1961.

Korb, Arthur. *How to Write Songs That Sell*. Boston: Plymouth Pub. Co., 1957.

Liehmohn, Edwin. *The Chorale*. Philadelphia: Muhlenberg Press, 1953.

Lookstein, Joseph H. "How Achieve a Sacred Image of Man?" *What is the Nature of Man?* Compiled by Religious Education Association. Philadelphia: Christian Education Press, 1959.

Lovelace, Austin C. and Rice, William C. *Music and Worship in the Church*. Nashville: Abingdon Press, 1960.

McMullen, John S. *Stewardship Unlimited*. Richmond, Va.: John Knox Press, 1966.

Meyer, Leonard B. *Emotion and Meaning in Music.* 9th impression. Chicago: University of Chicago Press, 1970.

_____. "Some Remarks on Value and Greatness in Music." *Aesthetic Inquiry: Essays on Art Criticism*

Miller, Robert William. *The Christian Encounters the World of Pop Music and Jazz.* St Louis: Concordia Pub. House, 1965.

Music in Church: Report of the Archbishop's Committee. Noel T. Hopkins, chairman. Rev. ed. Westminster, S.W.I.: Church Information Office, 1960.

Nelson, J. Robert. "Emil Brunner." *A Handbook of Christian Theologians.* Edited by Dean G. Peerman and Martin E. Marty. New York: World Pub. Co., 1965.

O'Connor, Elizabeth. *Eighth Day of Creation.* Waco: Word Books, 1971.

Parker, DeWitt Henry. *The Principles of Aesthetics.* New York: F.S. Crofts and Co., 1946.

Piston, Walter. *Counterpoint.* New York: W.W. Norton and Co., 1947.

Porteous, Alvin. *The Search for Christian Credibility.* New York: Abingdon Press, 1969.

Portnoy, Julius. *Music in the Life of Man.* New York: Holt, Rinehart and Winston, 1963.

Robinson, John A.T. *The New Reformation.* Philadelphia: Westminster Press, 1965.

Rosenberg, Bernard and White, David Manning, eds. *Mass Culture.* Glencoe, Ill.: Free Press, 1957.

Routley, Erik. *The Church and Music.* London: Gerald Duckworth and Co. Ltd., 1967.

_____. *Church Music and Theology.* Philadelphia: Fortress Press, 1965.

_____. *Music Sacred and Profane.* London: Independent Press Ltd., 1960.

Sayers, Dorothy L. *The Mind of the Maker.* Westport, Conn.: Greenwood Press, 1970.

Schaeffer, Edith. *Hidden Art.* 2nd printing. Wheaton, Ill.: Tyndale House Pub., 1972.

Seay, Albert. *Music in the Medieval World.* Englewood Cliffs, N.J.: Prentice-Hall, Inc., 1965.

Seerveld, Calvin. *A Christian Critique of Art and Literature.* Toronto: Association for Reformed Scientific Studies, 1968.

Smith, Charles T. *Music and Reason.* New York: Social Sciences Pub., 1948.

Stevens, Denis, and Robertson, Alec, eds. *The Pelican History of Music.* Vol. 1: *Ancient Forms to Polyphony.* Baltimore: Penguin Books, 1960.

Sweeney, James Johnson. "The Literary Artist and the Other Arts." *Spiritual Problems in Contemporary Literature.* Edited by Stanley Romaine Hopper. Harper Torchbooks/The Cloister Library. New York: Harper and Bros., 1957.

Thomas, George F. "Central Christian Affirmations." *The Christian Answer.* Editied by Henry P. Van Dusen. New York: Charles Scribner's Sons, 1945.

Thompson, Denys, ed. *Discrimination and Popular Culture.* Baltimore: Penguin Books, 1964.

Tinsley, E.J. "The Incarnation and Art." *The Church and the Arts.* Edited by F.J. Glendenning. London: SCM Press Ltd., 1960.

Trueblood, David Elton. *Philosophy of Religion.* New York: Harper and Row, 1957.

Urang, Gunnar. *Church Music—for the Glory of God.* Moline, Ill.: Christian Service Foundation, 1956.

Vaughan Williams, Ralph. *National Music.* London: Oxford University Press, 1963.

Verduin, Leonard. *Somewhat Less Than God: The Biblical View of Man.* Grand Rapids: Wm. B. Eerdmans Pub. Co., 1970.

Wentz, Frederick K., ed. *My Job and My Faith.* New York: Abingdon Press.

Wilkerson, David. *The Devil's Heartbeat: Rock and Roll!* Philipsburg, Pa.: Teen-Age Evangelism, n.d.

Wind, Edgar. *Art and Anarchy.* New York: Alfred A. Knopf, 1965.

PERIODICALS AND JOURNALS

Adorno, T.W. "On Popular Music." *Studies in Philosophy and Social Science* 9, pp. 17-23.

Allen, Peter. "The Problem of Communication." *English Church Music.* Croydon England: Royal School of Church Music, 1966, pp. 29-35.

Bahm, Archie J. "Creativity through Interdependence." *Southwestern Journal of Philosophy* 1 (Spring-Summer 1970): pp. 29-34.

Berlinski, Herman. "In Search of Criteria." *American Guild of Organists Quarterly* 10 (April 1965): pp. 55-59, 75-76

_____. "Pop, Rock and Sacred." Part II. *Music.* 5 (January 1971): pp. 46-50.

Brand, Eugene L. "Congregational Song: The Popular Music of the Church." *Church Music* (1968-1): pp. 1-10.

Bring, Ragnar. "The Gospel of the New Creation." *Dialog* 3 (Autumn, 1964): pp. 274-82.

Buszin, Walter E. "Luther's Quotes on Music." *Journal of Church Music* 13 (October 1971): pp. 2-7.

Cliburn, Van. "Great Music a Gift from God." *Arts in Religion* 19 (Winter 1969): pp. 3-4.

Cook, Robert A. "That New Religious Music." *Moody Monthly,* April 1977, p. 40.

Davis, Henry Grady. "Theological Foundations of Christian Worship and the Arts." *Response* (Pentecost 1959): pp. 4-8.

_____. "Theology in Relation to Arrangements for Music in the Church." *Response* 3 (Pentecost 1961): pp. 3-12.

_____. "Worship Music in a Synthetic Culture." *Concordia Theological Monthly* 33 (December 1962): pp. 733-37.

Dearnley, Christopher. "The Need for a Reformed Approach to Church Music." *English Church Music.* Croydon, England: Royal School of Church Music, 1969, pp. 23-28.

Elmore, Robert. "The Place of Music in Christian Life." *Christianity Today* 31 January 1964, pp. 8-9.

Halter, Carl. "Church Music as Art and Witness." *Journal of Church Music* 5 (December 1963): pp.2-5.

Holmes, Arthur F. "The Idea of a Christian College." *Christianity Today."* 31 July 1970, pp. 6-8.

Hunkins, Arthur B. "The Serious Contemporary Composer and the Church Today." *Music Ministry* 2 (1970): pp. 13-14.

Jones, W. Paul. "Art as the Creator of Lived Meaning." *Journal of Bible and Religion* 31 (July 1963): pp. 225-32.

Kaiser, Kurt. "The Trends of Performace in the New Music." *The Music Journal of the Southern Baptist Church Music Conference* 5 (1973): pp. 36-40.

Kobler, John. "Everything We Do Is Music." *Saturday Evening Post*, 19 October 1968, p. 46.

Lang, Paul Henry. "The Musician's Point of View." *Music* 2 (December 1968): pp. 34, 36, 38-39, 60-61.

____. "The *Patrimonium Musicae Sacrae* and the Task of Sacred Music Today." *Sacred Music* 93 (Winter 1966-67): pp. 119-31.

McLaren, Robert Bruce. "The Threat of Aestheticism." *Christianity Today,* 7 November 1960, pp. 16, 18.

Macquarrie, John. "What is the Gospel?" Part I. *Expository Times* 81 (July 1970): pp. 296-300.

Parvey, Constance F. "Christian Art in Mid-Century." *Response* 9 (Epiphany 1968): pp. 107-115.

Rookmaaker, H.R. "Letter to a Christian Artist." *Christianity Today* 2 September 1966, pp. 25-27.

Routley, Erik. "The Vocabulary of Church Music." *Union Seminary Quarterly Review* 18 (January 1963): pp. 135-47.

Sartin, Nancy E. "Toward a Musician's Theology." *Response* 7 (Pentecost 1965): pp. 9-13.

Schalk, Carl. "The Dilemma of the Contemporary Composer of Church Music." *Response* 7 (St. Michael and All Angels 1965): pp. 69-78.

____. "The Shape of Church Music in the '70s." Part I. *Journal of Church Music* 13 (October 1971): pp. 5-7.

Sherman, Franklin. "God as Creative Artist." *Dialog* 3 (Autumn 1964): pp. 283-87.

Sims, W. Hines. "What is Good Church Music?" *Church Musician* 2 (November 1951): p. 2.

Tangeman, Robert S. "Religion and the Arts: II, Music and the Church." *Union Seminary Quarterly Review* 12 (March 1957): pp. 55-60.

Thomas, T. Glyn. "The Relationship of Art to Religion: A Study of John Ruskin." *Expository Times* 82 (March 1971): pp. 182-85.

Tirro, Frank. "Choral Music." *Choral Journal* 8 (September-October 1967): pp. 20-21.

Wilder, Amos N. "The Arts as Interpreters of the Modern World." *Encounter* 28 (Autumn 1967): pp. 305-12.

Wood, Robert W. "The Aesthetic—A Forgotten Aspect of the Christian Life." *Japan Christian Quarterly* 28 (January 1962): pp. 22-36.

INDEX

absurdity   11

adventure   72, 75, 120

aesthetic theories   4-5, 64, 65

aestheticism   4-5, 109

aleatory music   11

ambiguity   72, 89*ff,* 91, 96, 100, 120

application of doctrines   111-121

appreciation (see music appreciation)

artist   10, 11, 15, 17, 23, 30, 53

artistic principles (see music composition, theoretical principles and universal artistic principles)

artistic vision   23, 37

arts   18, 23, 26, 27, 48, 65, 90, 91, 95, 96, 99, 103

arts, space and time   91, 93

arts and theology (arts vs. language)   90, 91, 96-101

asceticism   50

association   61, 70

athletic   84, 85

attitude   64, 80, 81, 84, 88, 114, 116

banal   (see cliché)

Biblical   (see Word)

business   (see commercialization)

church music, contemporary situation   3, 7, 20, 28, 29, 62, 73, 78, 82, 111, 112

church music, quality of   18-20, 24, 26-28, 57, 58, 80, 106, 107, 117, 119

church music program   13, 14, 16-20, 24, 27-29, 32, 39-41, 55-59, 86-87, 99-100, 101, 106-110, 111-121

church music witness   20, 24, 25, 28, 29, 62 (see musical witness)

cliché   18, 51, 54, 62, 91, 103, 119

commercialization   3, 19, 28, 47, 48, 49, 51, 52, 53, 54, 55, 56, 57, 60, 62

communication   34-39, 96, 98

communication, direct   36, 39

communication, indirect   37, 38-39, 40, 41

complacency   16, 17, 110

conformity   17, 18

congregational musical profile   34, 39-40, 111-113

consecration (see attitude)

contemporary music   54, 56-57

continuity   93, 94

contrafacta   50, 51

conversation, musical   111, 117

counterpoint   Prologue, 7, 8, 50, 87-88, 107-108, 111, 112-121

craftsmanship   15, 16, 18, 19, 118

creation   9, 18, 78, 103, 105, 116*ff*

creation, *creatio continua*   11-12, 13, 14, 76-77, 78, 117

creation, *ex nihilo*   9

creation mandate   12, 13, 16, 20, 21, 22, 27, 28, 95, 110

creative process   14, 15, 16

creativity   15, 16, 18, 19, 20, 22-24, 26, 28, 43, 62, 75, 76-77, 105, 106, 108, 109, 117, 119

creativity and the church   19-20, 103, 105, 116-117

creativity, definition of   15, 17, 19, 26, 43, 103

creativity, nurture of   16-17

creativity, objective phase   16, 18

creativity, standards of   19, 20

creativity, subjective phase   16, 18

crucifixion   102-103, 106, 107, 111

cultural accommodation 40, 49

cultural determinism 40

cultural mandate   12-14, 16, 17, 18, 20, 33, 117

culture   12, 13, 18, 36, 39, 40, 50, 62, 67, 73, 82, 83

delayed gratification   52, 72-75

dependence   9-10, 76, 79, 95

direct witness   36, 39

directional balance   108, 109, 110, 116, 118, 121

discipleship   44, 45, 46

discipline   44, 46, 81, 102-103, 104, 107

disobedience   23

doctrinal summaries   108, 109

dominance   94-95

dominion-having   12, 18, 21

education, music   52, 56-57, 75, 82, 83-85, 86-87, 116

emotion   64-65, 67-68, 70-71, 118

ends justify means   58-59

entertainment   34, 52, 70-71, 84, 104, 107

essences of life   97, 98, 99, 107

fact and truth   97-99

faith, the life of   63-72, 75, 118

faith action   71-75, 109

faith-walk   71-75, 108, 109, 111, 112, 113, 120

faithfulness   78, 79, 80

Fall   22, 23, 26, 27

folk music   59-60

form   10, 11, 15, 16, 18

form and content   30-31, 37-39, 41, 42, 118, 119, 121

freedom (see independence)

gospel, characteristics of   42, 43-46, 55

gospel, content and meaning   38, 39, 41, 42, 43-46, 119

gospel-folk   60

gospel song   56, 62, 70, 103

growth (see stewardship, growth)

history   13, 14, 102

holiness   78, 89, 90, 101, 120

humble exaltedness   10, 76, 109

humility   10, 31-34, 40, 102, 114

idolatry   70

imagination   15, 16, 18, 19, 94, 100, 104, 106

imago as a verb 25*ff*, 119

imago as creativity 21*ff*

Imago Dei 21, 43, 95, 105

Imago Dei, broad sense 21*ff*, 27, 116, 118

Imago Dei, narrow sense 24*ff*, 27, 105, 119, 120

immanence 11, 30*ff*, 90, 113, 114, 120

immediate gratification 52, 73, 74, 75, 100

incarnation 30*ff*, 36, 40, 102, 109, 113-114, 118, 119

incarnation, artistic 12, 16, 30, 31, 37, 38

independence 9, 10, 18, 94, 95

integrity 18, 19, 43, 44, 52-53, 54, 59, 60, 61, 109 (see craftsmanship)

intellect 64-67, 68-70, 71

intuition 16

jazz 59, 60, 61

judgments 19, 20, 95

judgments, objective 6, 80, 87, 109, 110

judgments, subjective 80, 83, 87, 109, 110, 117

kitsch 35, 47, 50, 52 (see mass culture)

knowledge precedes faith 35, 35, 71

language and theology (see arts and theology

law and grace 44, 45, 46, 81

listening 66, 74

love 30, 33-34, 77, 102, 107, 113, 114

mass culture 35, 36, 47-51, 62

mass production 18, 51

material world, goodness of 10, 11, 18

mediocrity 20, 23, 28, 52, 53, 79, 80

methodology 58-59

medium and message 37, 42, 55, 62

ministry (see pastoral musician and ministry)

music appreciation 40, 66, 83, 84, 85-87

music director (see pastoral musician and ministry)

musical composition 14-16, 68, 69, 70, 93

musical composition, theoretical principles 93-96, 100, 117

musical imaging (see redeemed imaging)

musical standards 19, 20, 28-29, 64, 81, 82, 84, 117, 119

musical witness 26, 28, 38, 42-43, 58, 59, 60, 61, 109, 119

muzak 48-49, 92, 104

mystery and music 89*ff*, 120

mysticism 125

newness (a new song) 18, 19

nurture 16-17, 18, 19, 84, 118

obedience 58

objective standards (see judgments, objective)

objectivity (see judgments, objective)

organic unity   37, 93, 94

originality   15

painting   38, 91

parable   38, 79

parable of the talents   79, 83

paradox   7-8, 71, 95, 97, 107, 111, 113

pastoral musician and ministry   Prologue, 3, 8, 31, 32, 33, 34, 40, 41, 62, 82, 84, 87, 88, 90, 95, 102, 108, 109, 110, 111, 114, 121

philosophical necessity   Prologue, 3

pilgrimage   18, 25, 73, 75, 83, 108, 120

pop music   3, 18, 62, 70, 74, 109

pop music, characteristics of 50-55

pop music, church   56-58, 62, 82, 119, 120, 121

pop music, definition of   51, 56

pop music, rationale for church use   57-59

pop musicians   57-58

popularity   46

pragmatism   5-7, 56-57, 58-59, 92, 109, 110

propaganda   36, 37

progress, congregational musical   112-113, 116

prophetic ministry   12, 13, 36, 90, 108, 109, 110, 113, 116, 117, 118, 119, 121

psychological attachments   85, 87

purpose   10, 11

redeemed imaging   26-29

redemption (see resurrection)

rehearsal   80, 81, 115

relevance, musical   35, 36, 110, 114, 117

relevance, verbal   35, 36

relevancy   34-36, 39-41, 109

renunciation discipline   103, 104, 106

responsibility   11, 12, 25, 44, 76-77, 119

resurrection   26, 65, 102, 104-107, 111

rock music   60, 61, 70

romanticism   44, 53, 118

sacred and secular music   63, 64, 65, 75

sacred-secular dichotomy   63, 64, 77

servanthood   31-33, 40, 109, 113, 114, 121

singing   18, 80, 81, 115

situationalism, musical   108, 109, 110, 111, 121

sovereignty of God   58, 79

standards (see musical standards)

stewardship   52, 76ff, 81

stewardship, doing one's best   45, 78-80, 80-83, 86, 87, 88, 115

stewardship, growth 83-85, 86-87, 116

stewardship, motivations for 76-77, 88

subjectivity (see judgments, subjective)

taste   19, 20, 84, 108, 117

teaching ministry (see education)

theology   7   (see   arts   and
    theology)

tradition   14

transcendence   89*ff*,   100,   109,
    120

trite (see cliché)

truth   Prologue, 41, 91, 92-95,
    109, 121

unified existence   63, 64*ff*, 68,
    71, 75, 77, 78, 94, 118

uniqueness   94, 95

universal artistic principles   38,
    92-95, 96, 100, 116, 117

value judgments   3, 7, 19, 20,
    74, 86, 117

variety   15, 94

witness, of a Christian   26 (see
    musical witness)

Word (Bible)   7, 8, 20, 30, 36,
    59, 84, 95, 96, 97, 99, 107,
    108, 109, 110, 111

working counterpoint   111-121

world-view   10, 11, 63, 92, 95,
    106, 117

worship   34, 66-68, 70, 72, 73,
    74, 83, 84, 86, 100, 106, 107,
    115, 118